C000291532

"Bronagh Starrs integrates psychological th[...]ical wisdom and profound empathy into a high[...] of anyone who cares for teenagers and their p[...] life through vivid case examples, a clear organi[...]ow to think about teenagers and the challenges t[...].his book is a gift to anyone looking to deepen their understanding of adolescent development and improve their clinical skills with teenagers and their parents."

Lisa Damour, *PhD,* **New York Times** *bestselling author of* **Untangled, Under Pressure,** *and* **The Emotional Lives of Teenagers**

"This book is a fantastic contribution to the field of adolescent psychotherapy. There are few who can match Starrs' depth of phenomenological attunement and degree of therapeutic sensibility with adolescents. She illustrates a masterful approach to understanding and supporting adolescents, capturing concrete therapeutic moments in vivid detail. Her engaging warmth and extraordinary humanity are evident on every page. Adolescent psychotherapists, irrespective of their approach, will find insights and applications to enrich their practice. A must-read for therapists, parents and anyone involved in the lives of teenagers."

Richie Sadlier, *bestselling author of* **Recovering** *and* **Let's Talk**

"This is a wonderful book that delivers a highly informative and useful relational perspective on adolescent configuration styles, parenting and psychotherapy. From beginning to end the book oozes rich and meaningful therapeutic experience and reflection on the challenges and opportunities presented when faced with adolescents who are primarily impulsive, inhibitive or directional in their interactions with the world. Importantly, how these styles develop and manifest is understood in the context of parents' own configuration styles, with constructive therapeutic solutions to dealing with specific adolescent/parent configurations explained in helpful detail. This is a must-read for anyone engaged in therapeutic work with adolescents, or in any other domain, and for parents, who often feel that they are in the dark when it comes to understanding their child's behaviour, and often don't see the role that they can play in how this manifests. This book helpfully shines much-needed light on these processes."

Dominic McSherry, *PhD, Reader in Psychology, Ulster University and Editor-in-Chief,* **Journal of Child and Adolescent Trauma**

"At last, we have a book which offers a framework for understanding the chaos of the teenager's psychological world, demonstrating to adults how to stay in contact with them. It should be read by therapists, parents and adolescents with similar fascination. Starrs' approach is very organic and human; validating the adolescent's subjective experience. She presents solutions which unfold naturally, in a flow of relational understanding. Her relational description of three configuration styles offers ground for therapy work. Parents reading this will understand why their good intentions don't bring expected results. Adolescents, themselves, might understand why they end up in negative loops of failure and resignation. Therapists and counsellors will find examples of gentle relational work, focused on emotional attunement as well as simple and straightforward concepts. Connecting feelings and behaviour with neurobiology of the brain, Starrs' work is directed towards development and growth, not on the pathology of adolescence. A joy to read."

Irena Bezić, *PhD, Co-founder of Centar IGW Zagreb Gestalt Institute, President of EAP (European Association for Psychotherapy)*

"The title of this book captures the process of becoming and being an adolescent and points to the movement involved – this is not a static stage of development. Bronagh captures the dynamic nature of adolescence with her exploration of adolescent configuration styles and parental responses, moving on to provide examples of therapy with parents and adolescents corresponding to the range of configurations. This is the descriptive part of my review of this insightful book, but there is more, Bronagh writes with great perception and wisdom and offers well-researched material including findings from neuroscience research to deepen the reader's knowledge. My reading of this book took me on a journey through the adolescent minefield and I was enthralled by the examples – they relate so well to my own experience of young people, as a professional and a parent of four. The way the book is structured, with adolescent and parental configurations, leads well to the final part on therapeutics. This is essential reading for all who work therapeutically with adolescents."

Sue Pattison, *PhD, Co-Editor,* **The Sage Handbook of Counselling Children and Young People**

Adolescent Configuration Styles, Parenting and Psychotherapy

Mental health has become the principal concern as adolescents struggle with a host of issues such as anxiety, academic pressures, gender, substances, social media, complicated family compositions and a vulnerable planet. This book provides psychotherapists with a clear theoretical understanding and practical application for navigating the increasingly complex adolescent experience as young people adjust and respond to the present-day world.

Starrs presents a contemporary understanding of adolescence, identifying three principal character styles and offering experience-near descriptions of the modern-day adolescent. The author demonstrates how each configuration style in adolescence elicits a predictable response in parents and examines the challenges and dilemmas facing parents in today's world, highlighting the patterns and pitfalls which often render parental interventions ineffective. Developmentally attuned parenting strategies are outlined, pertaining to each configuration style. The in-depth analysis of adolescent process and parental response has implications for the therapeutic encounter. Intervention focuses both on one-to-one work with the adolescent and parental involvement. The complexity of working with adolescents and parents who demonstrate psychological entrenchment is also outlined.

This highly readable, original and exceptional contribution is suitable for psychotherapists, allied professionals and parents alike.

Bronagh Starrs is creator and programme director of the MSc Adolescent Psychotherapy programme at the Dublin Counselling & Therapy Centre (Dublin) in partnership with University of Northampton. She maintains a private practice in Omagh, Northern Ireland and is the author of *Adolescent Psychotherapy: A Radical Relational Approach* (2019).

Adolescent Configuration Styles, Parenting and Psychotherapy

A Relational Perspective

Bronagh Starrs

Routledge
Taylor & Francis Group

LONDON AND NEW YORK

Designed cover image: © Bronagh Starrs

First published 2024
by Routledge
4 Park Square, Milton Park, Abingdon, Oxon OX14 4RN

and by Routledge
605 Third Avenue, New York, NY 10158

Routledge is an imprint of the Taylor & Francis Group, an informa business

© 2024 Bronagh Starrs

The right of Bronagh Starrs to be identified as author of this work has been asserted in accordance with sections 77 and 78 of the Copyright, Designs and Patents Act 1988.

All rights reserved. No part of this book may be reprinted or reproduced or utilised in any form or by any electronic, mechanical, or other means, now known or hereafter invented, including photocopying and recording, or in any information storage or retrieval system, without permission in writing from the publishers.

Trademark notice: Product or corporate names may be trademarks or registered trademarks, and are used only for identification and explanation without intent to infringe.

British Library Cataloguing-in-Publication Data
A catalogue record for this book is available from the British Library

Library of Congress Cataloging-in-Publication Data
Names: Starrs, Bronagh, 1970– author.
Title: Adolescent configuration styles, parenting and psychotherapy :
a relational perspective / Bronagh Starrs.
Description: Abingdon, Oxon ; New York : Routledge, 2024. |
Includes bibliographical references and index. |
Identifiers: LCCN 2023030803 (print) | LCCN 2023030804 (ebook) |
ISBN 9781032447223 (hbk) | ISBN 9781032447230 (pbk) |
ISBN 9781003373599 (ebk)
Subjects: LCSH: Adolescent psychotherapy. | Parenting. |
MESH: Psychology, Adolescent
Classification: LCC RJ503 .S716 2024 (print) | LCC RJ503 (ebook) |
DDC 616.89/140835–dc23/eng/20231006
LC record available at https://lccn.loc.gov/2023030803
LC ebook record available at https://lccn.loc.gov/2023030804

ISBN: 9781032447223 (hbk)
ISBN: 9781032447230 (pbk)
ISBN: 9781003373599 (ebk)

DOI: 10.4324/9781003373599

Typeset in Times New Roman
by Newgen Publishing UK

For Emily and Odhrán

Contents

Acknowledgements

My deepest appreciation and admiration go to the many adolescents whom I have had the pleasure and privilege of meeting, supporting and learning from over the years. My thanks also to the parenting adults who have entrusted these young people to my therapeutic care. Special thanks to those who have given permission for their stories to be represented throughout the book. Identifying information has been changed in order to ensure anonymity.

As adolescent psychotherapists we do this work so that, despite their struggles and traumas, the young people we meet might feel that they have a life that is worth living. I would like to thank all my colleagues, students and graduates for sharing in and nurturing my passion for this radically transformational time in people's lives. I continue to be inspired by their commitment to showing up for adolescents and my thinking has been enriched by our ongoing dialogue.

I am particularly grateful to Dr. Rosaleen McElvaney and Edel Quinn for their interest and generosity in reading the manuscript. The book has benefitted from their critical and considered feedback. I am also indebted to Maeve Lewis and Paul O'Donoghue for their continuing encouragement and guidance, and to Mark McConville, whose supportive hand at my back has made all the difference.

I wish to thank Grace McDonnell, editor, and Sarah Hafeez, editorial assistant, for their interest and support throughout the project. I would also like to acknowledge Lindsey Esplin, production editor, Carolyn Dodds, copyeditor, and the production team at Routledge for their thoughtful attention to the manuscript.

Finally, I owe a special and ongoing debt of gratitude to my family and friends for their limitless love, encouragement, availability and warmth. And this being the kind of book that it is, I wish to acknowledge the tremendous joy my adolescent niece and nephew, Emily and Odhrán, have added to my life, and to whom I dedicate this book. I could not love you more.

Introduction

This book explores how young people, their parents and their therapists experience the phenomenon of adolescing. Despite the mood swings, reckless behaviours, relentless overthinking and crippling anxiety, adolescence is not nearly as perplexing as adults perceive it to be. Fascinated by this stage of human development, I have made it my life's work to attempt to reach the heart of adolescent experience and help these young people more fluently navigate these years. In order to do so, I have paid close attention to the manner in which adolescents construct their worlds – identifying evolving patterns in their self-perception, contact style and behaviours during this time of radical transformation.

Having been involved in the training and supervision of many practitioners during my career, the one prevailing clinical dilemma which has most captured my interest is how to establish a developmentally transformative relationship with an adolescent. I hear therapists express the same binds over and over: *How do you talk to them? How do you get them to open up? When do you involve parents? What do you say to these parents? Why do my interventions fall flat?* Many therapists I talk to have a great capacity to develop rapport with young clients who, in turn, value the connection and keep showing up. However, all too often, these clinicians report feeling stuck in the work. Whilst the relationship has been well established, transformative potential is limited and developmental momentum is stalling. My first book *Adolescent Psychotherapy: A Radical Relational Approach* presents a developmentally and phenomenologically attuned methodology, offering strategic guidance to clinicians from the assessment process right through to specific clinical presentations and case management issues.

In this second book I frame the experience of adolescing as a progression through increasingly sophisticated psychological, emotional, behavioural and interpersonal levels of functioning. Development of the self during adolescence typically happens in three stages: 1) Boundaries from childhood and the adult world are established, behind which adolescents find ways to connect more deeply with peers whilst being motivated to do what they feel like doing. Self is experienced in relation to impulses: adults and homework are annoying; friends and gaming are cool. Peer-acceptance equates to self-acceptance as the interpersonal landscape is radically transformed. 2) The deepening of internal experience takes place, with a

DOI: 10.4324/9781003373599-1

narcissistic quality of self-absorption emerging in order to facilitate a deeper knowing of the self. Adolescents look inward in order to develop a stronger self-image, though without much psychological stability, it can feel like they are locked in a fairground hall of mirrors. Self, at this stage, is experienced with personal intensity and often with a good deal of insecurity and existential angst. 3) These prior stages of emerging selfhood set the scene for increasing self-assurance and lifespace balance as adolescents begin to have a deeper sense of security in who they are. Their increased psychological anchoring and self-possession extend to interpersonal contact and future planning. Whilst full adulthood is still a long way off, they are moving in the right direction. At least that is what we expect will happen…

The adolescent journey is fraught with trauma, complexity and inadequate lifespace support for many, and so the developmental trajectory is not always sequential nor does the experience of being a teenager unfold in coherent stages. Whilst each young person's lifespace is uniquely individual, over the years in my work as a psychotherapist, I have noted clusters of similar patterns, challenges and dilemmas which emerge for young people during the adolescing process. I refer to these clusters as configuration styles and have organised these into three principal configurations: *impulsive*, *inhibitive* and *directional*. In this volume, I present to the reader the essential features which are particular to each of these configurations. These developmental phenomena also tend to elicit predictable responses from parents, which can sometimes shape the parent-adolescent relationship in unproductive ways. For some young people these configuration styles map on to their developmental journey in a manner which resembles a stage model, as they move through each configuration in a temporal and sequential manner. For others, many of whom find themselves in a psychotherapist's office, they remain relatively entrenched in one or other of these configuration styles and may not progress through other configurations.

In recent years the field of neuroscience has shed more light on the science behind the art of psychotherapy, translating our experiential knowing into pragmatic description of the mechanics of nervous system functioning. These contributions have offered psychotherapists a rich lens through which to more deeply perceive the physiological, psychological and interpersonal changes which occur during adolescence. I remain fascinated in the mutually influential relationship between developmental experience and the adolescent brain. Drawing on this research in order to help adolescents, parents and professionals understand how the brain is developing and how this is both impacting on and is impacted by their lifespace experience, I find that it is best to keep the science very straightforward and uncomplicated. My reductionist approach, whilst overly simplistic, makes the knowledge accessible and supports the therapeutic enterprise. As a therapist, brain structures and functions are not foregrounded nor are they the central organising principle of my understanding and intervention. That said, I see the value of using neuroscience research to help explain psychological phenomena. From a therapeutic point of view, the aim is to informally and conversationally integrate some relevant neuroscience discoveries in order to foster curiosity, understanding and growth.

In these pages, I explore contemporary adolescent presentation and offer ways to support the healthy unfolding of developmental process. The principal aim of this book is to enhance therapeutic practice. Analysis of the contextual factors which shape the adolescing process is complex and, although fascinating for me, is the subject of other works. And whilst we know quite a lot, there is still much to determine about so many aspects of adolescence: the unevenness of development between boys and girls; why adolescents, in response to similar situations and traumas, creatively adjust in radically different ways; and why some adolescents become entrenched in self-defeating behaviours. As we continue to advance our knowledge of the factors which shape adolescent experience, this will enable us to develop increasingly attuned and effective adult-world responses.

The book is divided into three sections. Part 1 offers a description of configuration styles which I recognise as typical during the adolescent years, tracking the developmental features and challenges which are evident at various points throughout the adolescent journey. The opening chapters offer an experience-near description of the adolescent's developmental location, exploring the drives and developmental limitations of particular configuration styles and making sense of their often questionable and sometimes problematic presentation. Chapter 1 sets out the impulsive configuration style – with the draw to feel good and the seeking of validation within the peer landscape becoming figural at this stage. Childhood motivations are radically transformed, and self-acceptance is now equated with peer-acceptance as belonging becomes vital. The following chapter discusses the experience of entrenched impulsivity whereby adolescents become embedded in this configuration style, recycling through themes of indulgence and risk-taking, with the anticipated fallout and lack of developmental momentum. Struggles with mood dysregulation and limited self-discipline are documented. Chapter 3 offers a descriptive summary of the inhibitively configured adolescent who has a propensity towards self-conscious preoccupation and anxious rumination. Chapter 4 details the inhibitive adolescent's anxious lifespace which becomes infused with negativity and restriction, typical of so many teenagers in today's world. The final chapter in this section deals with the directional adolescent who has developed a degree of emotional and behavioural stability. For some adolescents this is evidence of psychological health and a strong sense of self; for others it is a creative adjustment to suffering.

Young people can be notoriously difficult to reach and influence during the teenage years and the experience can be challenging for parents at times. Part 2 explores adolescence from a parenting perspective, examining parenting styles and typical responses to situations and predicaments which frequently arise when raising teenagers. This section details commonly employed intuitive parenting strategies and outlines why they don't tend to be particularly effective. Parenting adolescents is not always a straightforward process and parents often find themselves at an impasse, not knowing how to help or influence their adolescent. It is at this point that psychotherapy is sought for the teenager, however mum or dad are usually also in need of support in order to transcend the powerlessness and overwhelm which has so often come to characterise their parenting experience. Involving parents in psychotherapeutic work, I have examined the dynamics of the adolescent-parent relationship and how teenage children are impacted by parental interaction. Over the years, having witnessed countless contact episodes unfold in front of me or having them described to me, after the fact, by adolescents or their concerned and exasperated parents, I have come to anticipate predictable, yet often unhelpful, intuitive parenting strategies. In Chapter 6, I provide a general overview of parents' configuration and contact style in relation to their capacity to attune to adolescent children. The following three chapters, in turn, explore the experience of parenting impulsive, inhibitive and directional adolescents, highlighting the issues and relational patterns which are distinctive to each configuration style. In order to skilfully assist their teenage children by implementing developmentally attuned strategies, parents require a level of insight, commitment and self-possession. In this section, I also explore how some parents themselves struggle as the result of the legacy of entrenched modes of being during their own adolescence and how this shows up in the clinical situation.

Part 3 focuses on therapeutics, demonstrating how to create a relationally and developmentally informed therapeutic space for both the adolescent and their parents. A trove of developmentally attuned macro interventions is offered. In this section I introduce *Sandspace*, a developmental technique I have created which supports the process for the adolescent, parent and therapist. Case vignettes are also included throughout in order to illuminate theory. Chapter 10 concerns therapeutic intervention with impulsive adolescents, supporting these young people to access greater consideration, discipline, self-reflection and choicefulness. After this comes a focus on parental intervention, exploring effective ways to guide parents to become more influential and to ensure richer relationship with their impulsive teenagers. Chapters 12 and 13 relate to the therapeutic enterprise with inhibitive adolescents, addressing the developmental dilemma of supporting these young people to shift from a posture of fear and passivity to adoption of greater ownership of their lives. The steps to support developmental momentum through engagement with parents of inhibitive adolescents are also outlined. Finally, Chapter 14 explores working with directional adolescents and their parents.

The reader will come to see that each configuration style in adolescence has a corresponding parenting strategy and distinct quality of therapeutic contact and style of intervention. As anyone who is attempting to parent, educate, mentor, engage therapeutically or support an adolescent in any other personal or professional capacity can attest to, a one-size-fits-all approach is inadequate in today's world. Our demeanour, our reactions and our approach when encountering a hell-raising, drug-taking party animal who could care less about his education are wildly different when we are faced with a highly anxious, overthinking perfectionist on the brink of an eating disorder; and different again when we are in the presence of a mature, balanced and resourceful inspiration whom we have to remember is still only fifteen. These days, parenting and therapeutic work require three principal levels of strategic approach depending on the developmental location of any given adolescent. That is a tall order!

This book is based on my clinical experience. The aim is not to situate it in a body of research, but to propose a framework based on that clinical experience which may be helpful for therapists working with adolescents. It portrays both the typical adolescent journey as well as the more problematic experience of entrenchment, exploring configuration dynamics and identifying relevant parental and therapeutic interventions. In sharing with the reader this way of organising understanding and intervention through the lens of configuration styles, it is my hope that this novel perspective will be clinically useful and transferrable to the clinician's own therapeutic practice. Attuned and rich contact with struggling adolescents and their parents can accomplish so much more than the reducing of symptoms or modifying of behaviour. Its transformative potential can support the reconfiguration of the adolescent lifespace in the direction of increasing integrity.

Part 1

The Adolescent

Chapter 1

The Impulsive Adolescent

Jamie is fourteen and impulsive. He comes in from school at four o'clock, drops his bag in the middle of the hallway and takes off his jacket, throwing it on the floor. He steps over it, kicks off his shoes and proceeds to the kitchen for a snack. Next the teenager opens the fridge, spies the cheese, then proceeds to hack off and eat half the block together with a bunch of slices of ham, finishing it all off with some orange juice. After this he heads upstairs to his bedroom, turns on his console, connects with his friends via his headset and starts playing his favourite game. Once it's finished, he plays another, then another. He's having fun!

His mother comes home at six o'clock and opens the front door. She starts muttering to herself:

'Look at the shape of this house! I might as well not have bothered tidying it last night. Jacket lying on the floor, as usual. I mean, the coat cupboard is literally beside where he dropped it. All he has to do is open the door and hang it up. It would take him two seconds. But no, not Jamie. It'll be lying there in a ball until the morning, unless I pick it up. And of course, he'll be running around looking for it and keeping the rest of us late as usual.'

Mum hangs up his jacket and walks on a few steps. *'I nearly broke my neck over those damned shoes of his. If I've told him once, I've told him a thousand times to put them away in the cupboard under the stairs when he comes in, instead of leaving everything lying around. I mean, how difficult could it be?'*

After putting away his shoes, she now eyes the schoolbag sitting in the corner. *'And look at the schoolbag sitting there unopened. This is his big year and that boy is going to have to buck up his attitude. I know where he is, upstairs playing that bloody Xbox. He's never off the damned thing. I'm sick telling him to get his homework done as soon as he comes in the door and then he can play it all evening. Nobody listens to a word I say in this house, I might as well be talking to the wall. The dog is the only one who pays any heed to me!'*

Mum opens the kitchen door to drop a bag of groceries on the table before going up to give him a piece of her mind and sees the remnants of Jamie's snack.

'Oh, for goodness sake, this isn't on. That's the lunch for the week. How could he not think? And he's drank straight out of the carton, so nobody else can drink the

DOI: 10.4324/9781003373599-3

orange juice now! Honestly, that boy thinks about nobody but himself. He doesn't give a damn about the rest of us, as long as he's alright. So bloody selfish.'

Increasingly frustrated, she walks upstairs and barges into his room. *'Get off that Xbox and get that homework done now! I'm sick and tired of telling you that if you don't start studying, you'll fail all your exams and throw your future away. And then where will you be? Don't roll your eyes at me, turn that damned game off when I'm talking to you. I'm going to throw that bloody Xbox out the window one of these days. And another thing…I had to lift your jacket and shoes, as usual. How many times have I told you to put them away when you come in? And you ate the food for the lunches for the rest of the week. I'm going to have to go and buy more. Do you think money grows on trees, do you? You have no respect for me or for this house. I'm out working my fingers to the bone all day. And for what? I don't know why I even bother. I come home and have to do everything in this house. Well, I'm fed up with it. Look at me when I'm talking to you. You've no manners and no respect for yourself or anybody else. You wouldn't have gotten away with this sort of behaviour in my day. And look at the shape of this pigsty of a bedroom. Disgusting. Get it tidied NOW!'*

Jamie tells mum he'll do his homework and tidy his room after this one game. She knows he won't. He doesn't.

According to his mother, Jamie is clearly the problem. There certainly is a problem…but is it really Jamie? Let's have a closer look, starting with what's happening in Jamie's brain…

The limbic system is located in the lower part of the brain and is the ground of our emotional world. When we respond to a thought, a person or an experience at a feeling level, our limbic system is deeply involved in this process – modulating the intensity of the feeling, such as happiness, sadness, fear or anger. The limbic brain is also fired up in relation to seeking pleasure, when our drive is to experience joy, satisfaction and delight. Not surprisingly, our limbic system is connected to sexual desire too. When the dominant activity in the brain is centred in the limbic region, adolescents tends to be impulsive. This means they are principally motivated by feelings, desires and urges. Later, they will develop the capacity to think these through and apply discipline to their choices. However, this may not happen for another few years.

Adolescence involves journeying through higher brain areas, as we acquire increasing sophistication, until we reach adulthood and become emotionally stable, highly self-aware human beings with excellent planning and decision-making capacities…here's hoping! But just now, at the beginning of adolescence, the limbic system becomes intensely activated whilst young people have little access to more evolved levels of functioning. This powerfully influences how they feel, think and behave. During this initial stage of the adolescent journey, two major dynamics shape the young person's experience: *feeling good* and *belonging*.

Feeling Good

Adolescents are now strongly disposed to *doing what feels good*: watching TV and YouTube videos, scrolling through social media, snapping eyebrows to friends, playing game consoles. Conversely, they are inclined to avoid what they *don't feel like doing*: homework, tidying bedrooms, stacking dishwashers, walking the dog (*their* dog which they pestered parents to get and for which they gave wholehearted assurance that they would take full responsibility).

Underlying this inclination to feel good is a heightened sensitivity to and more intense release of *dopamine*, a pleasure chemical in the brain. With dopamine young people feel happy, energised and focused. Without it they feel moody, aggressive and lacking enthusiasm. For example, fourteen-year-old Erin is super excited about the local teenage disco this coming weekend. She is in good spirits during the week at home, because of the dopamine surge which the anticipation of Friday evening has generated, chatting a little more than usual with her mother and being relatively obliging (also because she's put a request in for a new outfit for the disco). She invites her three friends round to get ready together and they all have a wonderful time on their night out.

On Saturday, Erin wakes up around lunchtime and sits on her phone – there's much activity on social media after last night. Several hours have passed, she's still in bed on her phone, dopamine is circulating and she's feeling good. Then her mum comes in (disgusted that her daughter has wasted half the day in bed – how anybody could sleep to that time is beyond her), opens the curtains, tells her to get up, strip the bedclothes, tidy and vacuum her room, bring down her laundry, take the clean laundry back upstairs and put it in her cupboards. This barrage of requests doesn't make Erin feel good – the dopamine stops flowing. She doesn't *feel* like doing any of these things, so she tells her mum to get out and she'll do it later. Her mother knows full well that Erin can't be trusted to do her chores, so after 20 minutes, she shouts up the stairs to remind her daughter to get up and get at it. The adolescent feels a little grumpy and assures mum, with a hint of aggression in her tone, that she will indeed do it – *just not now*. Both are becoming mildly frustrated and reactive. By the fourth time mum shouts up, a major battle ensues. Erin hates her very unreasonable mother whose sole purpose in life evidently is to make her daughter's life a misery. Shortly after this, her friend's mother picks her up and drops the girls into town. They browse around a few shops, have coffee and see a boy she likes. The dopamine levels are restored, and she feels good again. Erin begins to associate being around her mother with dopamine drain. She adopts a closed-down posture when they are together…unless that is, if she's in an especially good mood or wants something – then her mother is a wonderful human being and Erin is a joy to be around.

During these initial adolescent years, motivation is closely connected with feeling good. Erin's maths teacher, Ms Kelly, is strict and adopts a no-nonsense approach in her classes. When homework isn't completed, detentions are handed out and she has low tolerance for students not paying attention. Erin does not feel good in Ms Kelly's class and as a result, has little or no motivation to pay attention or do any work. Instead, she feels good talking to her friends during class and taking lengthy breaks in the toilets passing the time until the bell rings. Describing her experience, Erin says:

'Miss hates me, she picks on me for literally everything. I mean, I'm just sitting there doing absolutely nothing and she just shouts at me for literally no reason. She's the worst teacher in the school – everybody says so. I absolutely hate maths. I can't wait to drop it. I mean, when am I ever going to need algebra in my life? It's just so stupid and pointless.'

Erin fails her end-of-year maths exam quite spectacularly. Her report card reads: *Erin is inattentive in class and shows little interest in the subject. Has obviously done no revision for this test. Has potential; needs to apply herself.*

A new Irish teacher has been appointed to the school, Mr O'Doherty, straight out of college. He has a relaxed manner and is funny. Erin likes how she feels when she's in his class and has a crush on him. She loves Irish, remains focused in class, completes her homework and signs up for the summer Gaeltacht course. Describing Mr O'Doherty, she says: *'He actually treats us like real people and he's sooo nice. I love Irish and I'm thinking of becoming an Irish teacher.'*

She comes out near top of the class in Irish. Her report card reads: *Excellent result. Erin has plenty of ability. A pleasant and cooperative student.*

Next year, Ms Kelly retires, and the class get a new maths teacher – Mr Collins. He's young, hip and attractive. Erin loves maths now. Handsome Mr O'Doherty is replaced by Mrs Maguire, a battle-axe of the highest order. Erin hates Irish, refuses to study and is dropping it as soon as she can.

The adolescent's motivation is strongly tied to whether or not a person or situation makes her feel good and generates a dopamine release, which explains why younger teenagers allow their subjectivity about teachers to determine much about their academic life. As Erin progresses through secondary school, we expect to see an evolution in how she is motivated: by senior year, she may not like a teacher but commits to her studies regardless, as she needs good grades for college. But for now, if she doesn't like a teacher, best of luck getting her to take that subject seriously!

Belonging

Very often, adults don't respond to this new and natural dopamine-seeking stage favourably, and as a result, adolescents tend to experience them (especially parents, teachers and other authority figures) as judgemental, always on their backs and not a lot of fun to be around. Grown-ups tend to be seriously uncool and levels of embarrassment, especially caused by their parents, become more pronounced. This is why many would rather be seen dead than seen in public with mum or dad – like fifteen-year-old Kevin. He needs new trainers as he's growing so fast. His mum insists that they go into town, rather than purchase online, as she wants to have his feet measured. He protests strongly, tells her to just give him the money and he'll get them himself. She doesn't trust him to do that, of course. So, when he positively *has* to go shopping with her, mum is instructed to walk ten steps in front of her mortified son in town, for fear of him being spotted with her. Definitely not cool.

At the same time as this limiting of adult-world influence is evolving, social transformation with peers begins to unfold. Social acceptance is a strong generator of dopamine for adolescents, and much more central to self-identity than during childhood or adulthood. Childhood playmates are replaced with more intense and personally invested friendships as same-sex friend groups now become more gender diverse. These friendships take on greater significance as limbic activity drives young adolescents to seek validation within the peer landscape. Having friends and a reputation as being a well-liked kid are vital. Decent social status is the holy grail of early adolescence. In fact, at this stage, peer acceptability and belonging tend to upstage virtually all other aspects of their lives as associations with childhood activities are also dissolved.

Jack was a champion Irish dancer who had been dancing since he was five. It formed a central part of his childhood years and he loved it. Now that he's turned thirteen, Jack is refusing to go back. His parents try to convince him otherwise, bribing and bargaining with him, telling him how he'll regret it when he's older, to no avail. They don't understand – it was his passion and he's so talented at it? The official line to his parents is that he's quitting because he doesn't like it and doesn't want to do it anymore. Why? *Just because.* The real reason Jack has decided to stop dancing is because he's been taunted about being a girl and being gay by other boys in his class who have found out that he dances. Jack understands that Irish dancing is not cool, so continuing is not an option if he is to have a shot at peer acceptability and belonging.

Young people begin to feel more understood and accepted by their peers, and given the choice, most impulsive teens will opt to spend time with friends over parents. The developmental necessity to belong within the peer landscape is played out through face-to-face and social media contact, with both offering powerful pathways to connection or rejection.

Fiona was part of a friendship group all through first year in secondary school. As second year gets underway, she finds herself snubbed and on the margins, no longer invited to sit at the lunch table or participate in events happening outside of school. This devastates Fiona who quickly starts to dread going to school and cries herself to sleep on many occasions with the shame of being socially isolated. Fiona no longer belongs, and she has no idea know why. This peer dislocation results in the adolescent engaging in self-harm and presenting as relatively depressed. A young person can have wonderful adult support, great academic capacity and a generally supportive lifespace…but without friends, life can feel empty and meaningless. Acceptance and validation by peers are crucial and what really seems to matter at this stage is what contemporaries think, as the yearning to belong becomes a compelling influence on self-development.

As the significance of belonging within the peer landscape increases, so adults become even more hard to take. Conor's dad is giving him a lift into town. He hooks his smartphone into the car's audio system to play his music. He makes sure to select the most offensive music in his library – not that he necessarily wants to listen to it just now. Rather, he's looking for a reaction in order to amplify boundaries and create even more pushback. He actually finds it funny how much of a prude his dad is. Later that evening, the family go out for something to eat. Conor fancies the crème brûlée. He fancies the waitress too and is reluctant to ask for such a stupid gay-sounding dessert so instead orders his sister's chocolate brownie and instructs her to order his. One must be cool at all times.

For the impulsive teenager, romantic relationships, whilst often short-lived, can be characterised by intensity. The limbic brain offers a rollercoaster ride of shifting infatuation coupled with the allure of sexual arousal. It can be difficult for parents to accept that a beloved daughter, whom it seems like only yesterday was starting nursery school, has now developed sexual desires and is dating a boy one year older. She seems obsessed with him, wants to be with him all the time and her parents feel the intrusion into family life. What is more, they don't approve of him. After six weeks together, having fallen in love and identified as soulmates, the teenager has her heart broken because this boy has now hooked up with one of her friends. Two weeks later she's fallen in love again with someone else. Sex too, comes with its challenges. Transforming sexual arousal into choiceful sexual expression is a tall order. It requires quite a bit of brain functioning, namely the capacity to exercise inhibitory influence over impulses, as well as the planning and dialogue necessary to negotiate sexual desire, responsibility and mutual respect. *None* of these facilities are readily accessible during the early teenage years. What's more, the adolescent is further challenged by a wider world which promotes a boundaryless and highly sexualised culture of indulgence and desensitisation. The consequences of unconsidered and unprotected sexual activity and online exposure can be severe.

The Still-developing Brain

It is a universal yearning for any human being to want to feel good and fit in, though with dopamine surging and social acceptance equating to self-acceptance, impulsive adolescents are influenced by these drives in a more obvious and powerful manner than at any other point in their lives. This is because the early teenage brain does not yet have access to functions which keep these drives in check. All too often, this translates into choices and behaviours which are relatively unconstrained and undiscriminating, resulting in the impulsive-stage adolescent's lifespace typically characterised by chaos and trouble with a capital T. Let's take a look at what hasn't yet evolved in the teenager's brain at this stage of development.

Impulses, as we have seen, originate in the limbic system and take the form of feelings and urges. For example, Noah's younger sister is being annoying which generates an urge in Noah to thump her, which he does. His mother chastises him and takes his phone for the evening, which creates the urge to shout in her face about how much he hates her, then stomp off to his room, slamming his door loudly. He is infuriated that his mother refuses to listen to his side of the story: his sister was asking for it because she was annoying him on purpose. Mum *always* takes his sister's side. She *never* believes him, and Noah gets blamed for *everything*, just because his sister is the youngest and a crybaby. Developmentally, Noah has not yet achieved impulse control. His impulse centre is alive and vibrant, though discernment and conscious judgement are lacking. He has an impulse: his inclination is to indulge it.

Impulsive adolescents tend to forge connections with similarly impulsive peers – possessing a flair of finding friends with a twinkle in their eye, who are up for a bit of fun. Interestingly, it seems to me that parents are willing to blame the others in the friendship group as the bad influence – it's never *their* child! When Noah is with his friends, they vape, smoke weed and tend to binge-drink on nights out. When he's with his girlfriend and he's feeling sexually aroused, they sometimes have unprotected sex. When he's alone, his preferred activities are gaming, watching YouTube videos, gambling and viewing porn. His life is one big rollercoaster of dopamine hits. Noah's urges, which are often all-consuming, translate into actions without deliberation.

Noah does not yet have the capacity to *develop a relationship* with his impulses. That is to say, he does not possess the art of intuitively stepping back in a reflective capacity when an impulse emerges. In order to do this, he needs access to three mental elements which are not housed in the limbic system: *thinking*, *future-orientation* and *empathy*.

Thinking

To the outside world, especially the adult world, this is very straightforward – just think about your actions and consider the consequences! This involves mentally plotting out the potential process and inevitabilities of following through on his impulse. *If I do this, it might look like this and then that will probably happen because of it.* For example, in Noah's case…*If I hit my sister, she's going to start crying and run to mum who will take her side. Then mum will be mad at me and will take my phone off me again and I really want to chat to my girlfriend, so no…it's not worth it.* Thinking things through can put the brakes on impulsive decisions and young people are less likely to do things such as drink to excess, have unprotected sex or not bother with homework. As adolescents plot the points of where an action is likely to take them, the consequences of their impulse are revealed, and they can make an informed call as to whether following through on their impulsive course of action is worth it or not.

However, adults tend to forget very quickly what it was like to be an adolescent with an impulsive configuration style. The perennial question asked by adults to impulsive teenagers when they get in trouble is, *'What were you thinking??'* But they don't think; they *feel*. Their spontaneity means that they act on whim and it does not occur to them to engage in the art of reasoning. Despite the threat of adverse consequences, urges are translated into action without deliberation. They lack the skill to regulate what they *feel like doing* by responding through reason. Of course, they do actually possess the mental ability to think through their actions, though impulse tends to powerfully eclipse reason in these early teenage years. They're not stupid either, and there are also times when an urge is so overwhelming that they are very well aware of the recklessness of their actions, but they do it anyway – the feel-good is worth the fallout. (Have you ever walked into a shop and impulsively bought a bar of chocolate and ate it in two mouthfuls, despite the fact that you're on a diet, but you don't care in that moment because you *just want the chocolate*?) What is more, they can engage in hyper-rational thinking where they avert their gaze from any potential downside and actively support their impulsive urge. They are aware of the risk, but it won't happen to *them*. For example, as a young client and I are discussing choiceful sexual expression, Ellie informs me that she is not at risk of contracting an STI from her boyfriend. The adolescent reassures me that there is no need to worry: she trusts him implicitly. He's so lovely and he would never do that to her.

Future-orientation

A characteristic of healthy adulthood is that we can map out the future trajectory of an impulse decision. For example, if someone offers you the drug ecstasy, there are considerations: taking it will give you a peaceful feeling of self-acceptance; euphoria; absence of anxiety; an intense feeling of aliveness in your body; increased energy; and improved self-confidence. Let's face it – you'd be crazy not to take it! But then…you begin to weigh up the rewards and incentives against any anticipated future implications: you're not sure what's in the concoction and you've heard that people have become ill and even died from taking these kinds of things; there's a strong addiction history in your family and you don't want to play with fire; you've got to drive home and it's not OK to do so whilst high; you've got a really important meeting first thing and you don't want to be feeling the effects of taking ecstasy; the fallout of being prosecuted for possession of an illegal substance doesn't bear thinking about; and above all, you don't wish to use drugs. So, you say no – not because you don't want to feel all those wonderful things listed above, but because taking the drug has implications for both your immediate and long-term future.

The process is somewhat different in adolescence. Being future-oriented doesn't just mean weighing the pros and cons of future outcomes; it means considering the future in the first place. The impulsive adolescent typically doesn't compute like this and tends to make choices based on the momentary feel good factor. He is offered ecstasy and takes it because he loves the buzz and his friends are taking it too – it's going to be a great night! Thinking about the future tends to translate as far as: *Who has a free house this weekend so we can party?*

Considering the future and planning ahead are not part of the repertoire of an impulsive adolescent when it comes to decision-making processes. They do not tend to anticipate outcomes and consequences, nor do they have the realistic attainment of long-term goals forefront in their mind. These adolescents are disposed to having fanciful, and sometimes overly ambitious views of the future, such as the teenager with a less than mediocre following who wants to be a social media influencer and retire as a millionaire at 40, or who is getting below-average grades and has no academic motivation whatsoever, but who wants to study law at a prestigious university. These adolescents are full of good intentions when it comes to the immediate and long-term future: they'll start studying; they'll stop vaping; they'll tidy their rooms; they'll cut the grass; they'll get off their phones; they'll wear condoms. They definitely do intend to do these things, they really do…but just not right now, because they don't *feel* like doing them. However, the future will sort itself out favourably, and with little effort.

Sometimes the stakes are very high in relation to impulsivity and a young person's future, particularly with regard to medical issues. Fourteen-year-old Blain was diagnosed with type 1 diabetes as a youngster, which necessitated relentless supervision of blood sugars and created tremendous upheaval to family life. Throughout childhood his parents took responsibility for the management of his condition and approached the task with diligence, despite feeling overwhelmed. With adolescence on the horizon, the balance of power has shifted, and Blain's parents have had to begin to play a different role in relation to supervision of his medical treatment and daily eating habits. The adolescent has demanded that they back off as he has taken over the reins. Unsurprisingly, impulsive teenagers who live with health conditions demonstrate concerning levels of noncompliance – and Blain is no different. His cooperation and childhood compliance have been replaced by neglect and intransigence. Governed by feelings, he is sick and tired of having to negotiate the condition every day of his life and instead lives now as if he no longer has diabetes – because he *doesn't want* to have it anymore. Having been referred for therapy, I meet the adolescent via an online platform. Behind him on the screen, along the length of his bedroom window, sits a neat row of empty high-sugar energy drinks which he has collected. As we unpack the meaning of this, he acknowledges that it is a symbolic one-finger salute to his parents who never shut up about his goddamn blood sugars. Blain's health is already starting to become compromised through his reckless relationship with diabetes, which becomes even more problematic when he adds alcohol into the mix…but he doesn't care. His parents perpetually nag and warn him about the complications associated with diabetes and that if he continues on his destructive path, he could become seriously ill or die by age forty. He finds this both comical and pathetic: he doesn't care about living beyond forty – that's so old! Besides he just cares about having fun *now*.

Empathy

Empathy is the capacity to conceive of the experience of another person – their thoughts, feelings and behaviours – by stepping imaginatively into their perspective. This is a sophisticated process and an integral element of healthy adult relating. It can be a little trickier for impulsive-stage adolescents whose self-reflective capacity is limited, never mind their capacity to perceive anyone else's inner world. Peter's father typically picks him straight after school, except on football practice days when his training ends at half past four. The adolescent isn't sure if he has football after school today or not, he can't remember what the coach said. They agree that Peter will call his dad to let him know what's happening after school. Dad stresses the importance of the call, reminding his son that he's busy and his time that day is very tight. Peter feels nagged and treated like an idiot as his dad prattles on and on about it. His responses escalate in frustration from *'Yeah'* to *'Okayyyy'* to *'Rightttt'* to *'Oh my God…I heard you the first time. Seriously??'*

Peter doesn't call. It turns out he does have football practice this evening, but he doesn't consider his dad in the situation. Without access to empathy, Peter doesn't imagine how grateful his dad will be at the thoughtful call which means he has an extra hour to complete his tasks; neither does he consider how vexing it will be for his dad to have to sit unnecessarily at the school gates wasting an hour waiting on his son, when he's got so many work commitments. Dad is exasperated when all of the students pile out through the school gates and Peter is nowhere to be seen. When the adolescent finally saunters towards the car after football practice, he's met by an agitated father: *'You were meant to call! Why the hell didn't you call and tell me that you had football practice?'*…to which Peter responds simply and truthfully, *'I forgot.'*

His father's predicable next question is, *'HOW could you forget?'*

Peter answers, *'I dunno; I just forgot.'*

On the journey home, Peter gazes out the window, intermittently rolling his eyes whilst dad is on a rant…something about 'attitude' and 'selfish' and 'thinking about other people'. The adolescent reminds himself what an insufferable idiot his dad is.

Attuning to others can mean inhibiting an impulse to feel good, feel powerful or to be funny – and that's a non-starter for some of these teenagers. Louise is spending the day with her mother and aunts at a show in Dublin. During the interval, her mother hands her phone to Louise and asks her to text her brother Cian, who is at home by himself, whilst mum goes to get ice cream for everyone. *'Just ask him how he's doing and tell him we'll pick him up some food on the way home.'*

Louise takes her mother's phone and texts: *You were a mistake.*

When she realises what has happened, her mother is horrified and phones to explain the text to her bewildered son. Louise thinks it's hilarious.

The allure to do whatever it takes to feel good becomes muted as adolescents progress through more sophisticated brain functions, however when the limbic system is strongly activated, it's challenging to resist this temptation. Impulsive-stage teenagers will lie and cheat to feel good, not giving a thought to or caring sufficiently about the impact of their actions on others. Sinead vapes, because it makes her feel good and look cool. She regularly concocts stories about needing money for school activities in order to buy resources, despite an awareness that money is tight at home. Her mother reluctantly gives Sinead a few euros, explaining to the adolescent that it is all the money she has in her purse, then proceeds to show her daughter the empty purse. Mum's soft heart means she is gullible, which works perfectly to the adolescent's advantage. Her appeals are lost on Sinead. As she is expressing her financial concerns (knowing there is a definite possibility that Sinead is blatantly lying to her but giving her the benefit of the doubt) the adolescent is thinking to herself: *What a drama queen. Just give me the money, for God's sake!* Sometimes it's easier for the adolescent to simply pinch a few euros from her mother's purse when no one is around. She just wants to vape, and other scenarios don't occur to her, such as the thought of her mother struggling to make ends meet. On multiple occasions mum opens the door to her daughter's bedroom and is met with a sweet smell and haze of smoke. Sinead reacts with indignation and anger to the accusations that she has been vaping. When mum one day finds her vape and confronts her, the adolescent assures her that she is holding on to it for a friend and categorically denies it is hers. She is incensed that her mother never trusts her. How dare her mother accuse her. It isn't fair, Sinead gets blamed for *everything*!

A Note on Bullying

Much bullying behaviour relates to limbic system functioning, as empathy is essentially offline, and these kids are not thinking about the implications of their actions. Whether the bullying mode is verbal, physical, cyber or exclusionary, the one thing these experiences have in common is that they make the aggressor feel good, feel powerful, be funny or belong – and the result is often an elevation in peer status. That this comes at the cost of another peer's happiness, belonging, sense of self or even their life, is of little concern.

Harry attends an all-boys school and is easily singled out due to his shy, quiet, slightly backward manner. In truth he is a lovely young lad, though he doesn't stand a chance with his peers. The particularly impulsive ones make his life a misery on a daily basis for five years until he finally leaves the school. They taunt him about his appearance, about being gay, make cruel jokes whenever they can, repeatedly push, trip and block him as he makes his way around the school and post humiliating rumours online. Every now and again some of the boys tackle him to the floor, hold a phone to his face and force him to watch gay porn clips. Harry sometimes considers suicide as a solution for putting an end to the torturous intimidation he endures. When I meet him, he has accumulated so much distress during his secondary school years that he has Post-Traumatic Stress Disorder.

Tragically, bullying is a pervasive modus operandi within the adolescent world. The behaviour, whilst inexcusable, is understandable when we view it through the lens of limbic activity. A number of years later, Kai, one of Harry's oppressors, comes to me for therapy. He feels depressed, is smoking way too much weed and has failed the second year of college. Kai knows that he needs to deal with issues from his past, including the experience of growing up with an alcoholic dad and enduring the fallout of a particularly hostile parental separation when he was twelve – just around the time he started secondary school. In the course of our work, the adolescent mentions feeling shamed about how he treated a kid in his class and mentions Harry. Kai was one of the main perpetrators of Harry's persecution. He describes how he would say something comical and demeaning about Harry to make the others laugh. These moments would reinforce his identity as being 'really funny' and create a stronger sense of belonging for himself within his peer group. Kai would also feel good and feel empowered, so there were plenty of benefits for him in continuing his daily assault against Harry. The adolescent's creative adjustment to family adversity was to feel good and to belong in school. Whilst this was a healing and life-giving experience for the adolescent in the face of a miserable home life, and probably made all the difference during his teenage years, his approach created harm. Kai's description of the difference between home and school is striking:

'When I was with my dad, he just got drunk and yelled all the time. Mum was always crying or talking to her sisters. They never shut up about much they hated each other. It was a nightmare. School was a saviour. I had so much fun and my friends were brilliant. I would go in every day and it would be the best laugh from start to finish. It kept me sane.'

Kai sees now that their relentless persecution of Harry was an effective process through which he and his impulsive friends advanced their status and belonging. Every time they acted or colluded against this struggling and isolated teenager, they cemented their position as socially acceptable and 'not like Harry'. There were times Kai felt a little guilty and uneasy about Harry's treatment, though to stand up and call out this behaviour would be social suicide.

People sometimes do terribly unkind things to others when limbic energy is dominant, when empathy is not readily accessible and peer belonging is so much at stake. Impulsive teens can find it difficult to inhibit behaviour, which is insensitive, inappropriate or rude, and take things too far *without thinking*. Thankfully most people progress beyond this stage and become caring, empathic, responsible citizens. As a twenty-year-old, Kai is now feeling remorse and mortification.

The Problem with Jamie...

Having explored some features of the impulsive configuration style, such as the investment in feeling good and the urge to belong; and the struggles with access to thinking, future-orientation and empathy, in the face of such powerful impulses; let's return now to Jamie whom we met at the start of this chapter.

He is in his bedroom happily playing his game console before his mother so rudely interrupts with her nagging. Here's a recap of the adolescent's experience: Jamie is fourteen. He comes in from school at four o'clock, drops his bag in the middle of the hallway and takes off his blazer, throwing it on the floor. He steps over it, kicks off his shoes and proceeds to the kitchen for a snack. Next the teenager opens the fridge, spies the cheese, then proceeds to hack off and eat half the block together with a bunch of slices of ham, finishing it all off with some orange juice. After this he heads upstairs to his bedroom, turns on his console, connects with his friends via his headset and starts playing his favourite game. Once it's finished, he plays another, then another. He's having fun!

We can see that Jamie is developmentally on point – doing what he *feels* like doing, not thinking about the future implications of his actions, displaying no empathy for other family members and being solely invested in making himself feel good. His configuration style is unmistakably impulsive. His mother understandably is not impressed with how he is conducting himself and has somewhat unrealistic expectations of her son. Here's what she wants to see happen:

Jamie comes in from school, takes off his blazer and kicks off his shoes. Then it occurs to him that if he neatly places them in the hallway cupboard it will keep the place tidy and he'll know exactly where they are in the morning. You see, he doesn't like to keep his mother late for the school run as the cascade effect of this is that she ends up late for work, so he's super organised when it comes to his morning routine, with his great sense of responsibility and team effort within the family. He then becomes aware of feeling peckish, though Jamie doesn't want to ruin his dinner, so he decides between waiting until dinner time or maybe having something light and healthy. He opts for a small salad, prepares it and returns the kitchen to its former state before heading upstairs, because that's the considerate thing to do. He feels like playing his game console and chilling out after the long school day; however, he is aware that if he completes his homework now, he'll be able to fully relax and have the whole evening to himself after it's done. And his homework is important because this is an exam year. He understands that if he puts the work in now, he's investing in his academic future. He also knows that it will please his mother greatly, so he does exactly this. As Jamie is concentrating on his studies, his mind meanders to his mother. He thinks empathically and compassionately about how hard she works all day and how she has to come home and make the dinner for everyone, do the laundry, help with homework and how she generally never has a chance to sit down. She really is a tower of strength – a selfless and inspirational woman, he thinks proudly. He is moved by his empathic resonance, takes a break from his study and goes downstairs to peel the spuds. He thinks to himself that at least that's one less thing his mum has to do this evening. Afterwards, the adolescent resumes his study and at six o'clock hears his mother coming home. He meets her in the kitchen and has an emotionally articulate dialogue with her about how his day went and asks about hers, in the middle of which, he offers to make her a cup of tea.

His mother's demands for Jamie to buck up his attitude will require a brain transplant!

Due to the fact that impulsive adolescents don't come with a user manual for parents, his mother doesn't quite get that Jamie's limbic system is the dominant functioning area of his brain, shaping why he does what he feels, without thinking. She yearns for him to have better decision-making and problem-solving capacities and improved reasoning ability, as family life would be so much more peaceful. However, with this gap in her understanding, Jamie's mother perceives her son's behaviour as being an attitude problem and describes him as both lazy and immature. For this reason, adult-world reaction to impulsive adolescent behaviour is commonly antagonistic and alienating. We'll explore this later in the book.

At fourteen years of age, connections between the limbic region and other parts of Jamie's brain are still developing and will continue to do so until he's in his mid-twenties. In time, he will *hopefully* demonstrate a capacity to self-regulate, becoming organised, attentive, empathic and able to carefully consider his decisions. Just not for the first few years of his life as an adolescent. For now, with little capacity to contain his drive to feel good, to think about his actions and make decisions based on optimal outcomes, we might expect poor academic motivation, behaviour influenced heavily by peers, risky experimentation with alcohol, drugs or sex, and an untidy, smelly bedroom.

Looking back, we are sometimes astounded that we survived adolescence, given our recklessness and the crazy situations we found ourselves in. Thankfully, the universe is kind to adolescents, and most emerge from the impulsive stage with only a few minor scrapes, occasional shame-shivers and the question, what was I *thinking*??

Chapter 2

Entrenched Impulsivity

The descriptions so far in this section relate to developmental impulsivity, that is to say, the typical impulsive presentation we expect to see from younger teens. However, some people remain caught in an impulsive lifespace and do not progress to more reflective, choiceful, matured ways of being later in their adolescence and often right throughout their adult lives. In these situations, the lifespace is characterised by dysregulation, reactivity, chaos and addiction. This entrenchment is commonly present from childhood and limbic activation has already been the dominant approach to life long before the teenager begins to emerge. Still others have given little cause for concern during childhood, only to 'go off the rails' in adolescence.

Adolescents who exhibit entrenched impulsivity typically live their lives through emotional reactivity and don't quite reach the stage of being able to moderate their urges through reflection and bigger picture thinking. Compared with their counterparts, their impulses appear amped up and this leads to powerful and unbridled instincts which the adolescent is hellbent on satisfying, such as *having* to get new trainers and going into a full-blown rage attack if their demand isn't met immediately, or always taking a night's drinking way too far. Patience, discipline and flexibility are not in their repertoire. Instead, these adolescents struggle with not getting what they want in the moment, demonstrating little or no personal accountability and are driven by a strong urge to feel good. This remains their default position as they progress through their adolescent years and beyond.

Impulsive teens are spontaneous and ready to jump right in with both feet at a moment's notice, if the payoff is feeling good or belonging. The downside is that planning is usually not part of this process, so outcomes can be dubious. To be sure, a spontaneous spirit lands lots of teenagers in hot water and can be like walking into the lion's den, but with impulsivity at extreme levels, it's like meeting the entire pride. I'm reminded of nineteen-year-old Claire who decided on a whim to head to London, booked a flight and arrived with a backpack later that day, twenty-five euros in her account and nowhere to stay. She ended up meeting a group of squatters and spent a week smoking weed and playing guitars with them until her parents eventually tracked her down.

DOI: 10.4324/9781003373599-4

These adolescents demonstrate intense excitement about new friendships, ideas or projects – working themselves up into a frenzy of passion, only to disengage and grow bored as soon as the appeal wanes – precisely at the time when real commitment and discipline are called for. Eoin's home is filled with evidence of passionate beginnings which fell by the wayside: a keyboard and drum kit, tennis and badminton rackets, a set of golf clubs, a martial arts suit, as well as chickens and a goat which his mother now tends are just some of the items in his collection. His parents bring him to see me because he has recently announced that he is going to be a dad. He had had a drunken one-night stand with a girl he knew. She is going to keep the baby and he will support her and be fully involved in raising the child.

Already by twenty-two years of age, Eoin has created a chaotic trail in his life. He is bright but hated school, so didn't study and as a consequence left with few qualifications. He has been in numerous jobs since then, over a dozen at least, and either left or was sacked from each one. In the few months that we work together, he goes through three different jobs. Each new position is 'brilliant' and Eoin is brimming with enthusiasm – but inevitably something always spoils it for him: the boss, the hours, the pay, the effort, the monotony, the customers, the days missed, the hangovers…and it is time to move on to the next job. Taking no responsibility, he justifies with each one why it is right for him not to have stayed.

We have an idea in our minds of how a twenty-two-year-old ought to show up in the world, though entrenched impulsive adolescents present as much younger and more immature. Working with Eoin is like working with an impulsive thirteen-year-old. Much of his dialogue is focused on giving out about how annoying his mother is as she nags him every morning to get up for work and treats him like a baby. He avoids taking ownership of the fact that he is failing to manage these basic daily tasks on his own. Eoin sounds impressive in relation to his imminent role as a new father – he speaks about how seriously he takes his responsibilities, and how he is going to make it work with this girl. He proposes to her and they move in together almost immediately. As all this is unfolding, the adolescent begins a covert relationship with another young woman who has a six-month-old baby, having left her partner two weeks after meeting Eoin. When the situation is discovered, both relationships end, he moves back home and goes on a drinking binge with his friends. This ends with him being sacked from his new job for failing to show up. His contact with his daughter remains sporadic.

The Emotional World

Emotional storms and explosive outbursts are characteristic due to the fact that adolescents who experience entrenched impulsivity tend to have very low thresholds for arousal and are easily provoked to anger. Sometimes they experience 'blind' rage where they say and do things which cause harm and upset – because they are wholly consumed by their feelings and are not thinking about their behaviour. They have little capacity to stop, reflect and tone down their reactivity. They 'just lose it'. At other times, adolescents are aware and report feeling that they just don't care about the consequences. For example, Lewis describes roaring at his mother and pushing her during an argument. He tells himself to stop shouting but he feels compelled to continue as he likes the feeling of power he is experiencing. The more out of control he senses he is becoming, the more powerful he feels. Add alcohol to the mix and outbursting is even more likely. The joint pursuits of drinking to excess and getting into fights can become regular features of nights out for some.

These adolescents tend to struggle making transitions from enjoyable activities to more mundane tasks, such as being asked to stop playing their games console in order to pack their schoolbag or have dinner with the family. The teenager will become easily frustrated and irritable, and this reasonable request can morph into a protracted and explosive rage attack. They can also have great difficulty negotiating difficult feelings, such as losing, disappointment and making mistakes. Their poorly regulated emotional world will express these as irritability, aggression and blaming others. For example, Sean loves playing his game console, but cannot tolerate losing. Whilst it's typical to hear gamers in upstairs bedrooms swearing loudly and banging their feet on the floor when they're beaten, Sean has, several times, fractured bones in his hand punching his bedroom wall and smashed countless controllers against it.

This is entrenched impulsivity, where not feeling good is intolerable. This creates a scenario where adolescents live life essentially on their terms. These adolescents are defiant, do not comply with rules and intensely dislike being subordinated by adults. When things don't go well, they typically display aggressive behaviour and may make threats of violence. The strength of an unconstrained emotional field, the propensity to reactivity and the fact that empathy is offline makes for a concerning profile, which makes it possible to dehumanise and objectify another person and treat them with cruelty. When taken to the extreme, sadistic impulses emerge, where suffering and humiliation are inflicted on other people or animals for the purposes of deriving pleasure.

School

Probably all impulsive teens struggle with aspects of school and can be a bit of a handful to manage in the junior years of secondary education, though most will navigate the experience without too much adversity, save for a few report cards which make unimpressive reading. However, some who exhibit entrenchment will find it much more problematic. With an expectation to sit quietly, pay attention, concentrate on uninteresting topics, engage in tasks which require alertness and sustained effort, and exhibit socially appropriate behaviour, school typically proves a challenge. Skipping school is common, however in sharp contrast to anxious teenagers who don't attend but who want to be in school and are academically engaged, these adolescents are seeking to avoid the boredom and punitive culture of day-to-day life in a secondary school. *Sit down. Stop talking. Stop swinging on that chair. Put that phone away. Pay attention. Where's your homework? Are you listening to me? It's your own time you're wasting. Come up to the front so I can keep an eye on you. Go to the principal's office. You're in detention for a week.*

School is often a place of failure, where they are constantly in trouble and struggle with the demands of having to pay close attention to subjects which they find incredibly boring and irrelevant. Instead, they are easily distracted, fidgety, chatty, defiant, disruptive and often adopt the role of the class clown. It's difficult to organise your school day, remain on task, follow through on instructions and spend several hours on homework and revision when your motivation levels to do so are at zero. The school experience for adolescents whose limbic system is dominant and formidable tends to be awash with shame and can be a bit of a nightmare for all involved. Adolescents who endure entrenched impulsivity tend to be familiar visitors to the principal's office and are regularly threatened with detention, suspension and expulsion.

Following the transition from primary to secondary school, Cillian is finding the interruption of moving between classes difficult. He constantly talks and pesters his peers, is unable to follow direction and walks around the classroom when the notion takes him. During momentary episodes of interest, he blurts out answers and has difficulty waiting his turn. Teachers do their best to manage his behaviour, but their efforts lack much influence. When confronted and held to account about his behaviour, Cillian becomes verbally and physically aggressive – punching, kicking, swearing and running away. He demonstrates contempt for authority figures. When I meet him, he is on the point of being expelled. His mother is desperately worried about his safety and his future. Cillian isn't. He just hates school and wants to leave. The threat of expulsion is a gift and when his mother expresses her concern about how he is throwing his life away, Cillian sniggers scornfully. He couldn't care less.

Friendship

Friendship qualities such as reciprocity and mutuality are beyond the excessively impulsive adolescent's capacity, which limits the possibilities for healthy interactions. Some are great at making friends, but struggle to hold on to them. Tracking the impact of their moods and behaviours on other people is a difficult task. Because of this, they exhibit bossy and sometimes outrageous behaviours and can have considerable problems maintaining peer relationships. They are entertainment for classmates, but their brazenness and excessive risk-taking mean that they tend to be overlooked when it comes to birthday celebrations, sleepovers and other close friendship activities. There is a reluctance to be closely associated with very impulsive teens and their over-the-top antics, as peers know that keeping company with them is likely to get them into trouble. The risk is that they will simply take things too far. Their volatility can also be intimidating, and other teenagers aren't always comfortable being around them. At the same time, their yearning to be accepted and belong is present despite poor social etiquette and awareness of the social implications of their impulsivity – and just like their less impulsive peers, they have a keen sensitivity to social rejection and isolation. This aspect of life can be very painful for them. Alternatively, if a group of adolescents who demonstrate entrenched impulsivity come together in friendship, it is likely that the stakes will be high in relation to dopamine seeking. In these instances, the buzz is often generated through antisocial activity.

Sex

The limbic region is central in mediating sexual arousal. Parental conversations about the topic or sex education programmes attempt to encourage young people to apply thinking, future-orientation and empathy to their sexual urges. As we have seen, this is a tall order for the impulsive teen. Porn, on the other hand, is a much more pleasurable and accessible mode of sex education, although its modelling of consent, mutuality and safe-sex practices are controversial and problematic. For many, disconnection between sexual satisfaction and being in relationship is normative. Over-reliance on pornography, with all its implications, has become a common feature of adolescent sexual expression. There are risks for some excessively impulsive adolescents whose general approach to satisfying their urges and getting their needs met is to demand, push and pressure. This can translate into sexual harassment and engaging in compulsive or abusive behaviours in order to satisfy the sex drive (their sexually harmful behaviour may also be connected with entitlement, aggression, power and substance misuse). For others, entrenched limbic activation and the underdeveloped capacity to consider risk and consequences results in heightened sexual vulnerability. The stakes are high, with the possibility of sexual assault, sexual health risks and pregnancy for these young people, such as fifteen-year-old Ellie who hangs out with much older adolescent males. When they meet up, they drink and smoke weed together. Sexual encounters with different members of the group are commonplace. Ellie has no sense that she is being exploited and has no idea how to keep herself safe. Belonging in the group comes at the cost of her integrity and she confuses their sexual attention with their care for her.

Addiction and Criminality

Impulsive-stage adolescents have an experimental nature and may get drunk or dabble in drugs. However, there is a hard-core approach when it comes to entrenched impulsivity: experimentation with alcohol, drugs and other highs or feel-goods can all too easily move into the world of dependency, addiction and loss of control. Unconstrained impulsivity means that feelings govern thoughts and actions, which is why these adolescents are in search of pleasure and highs, and struggle with the mundane or uninteresting. Their cavalier, reactive attitude to life may well have repercussions. For some, byproducts of the chaos trail their lifestyle creates include shame, regret, depression and suicidal impulses. Being in trouble with adults can get upgraded from parents nagging and being sent to the principal's office, to engagement with the criminal justice system and incarceration. Young people in the criminal justice system overwhelmingly endure entrenched impulsivity and are punished for it. As we will see later in the book, punishment does not create the developmental transformation necessary for higher regions of the brain to function optimally, which likely contributes to why reoffending rates are so high.

At twelve years of age, Jake rarely went to school and his binge-gaming bordered on addiction. He started drinking and soon progressed to cannabis, then on to hallucinogens and cocaine. Through his teenage years, drug dealing and stealing became ways of supporting his addiction and also gave him status for a while. A number of his friends died by suicide and from overdoses or accidents. By late adolescence, his life was defined by his addictions and a criminal record. He had a complete lack of ambition and no plans for the future. Jake was depressed and had attempted suicide several times when I met him. Developmentally appropriate limbic activation is a healthy stage in the process of becoming a self, but the outcomes are detrimental and sometimes catastrophic when experienced excessively.

Diagnosis

When the limbic system is in the saddle and dictating the terms of a young person's engagement with the world, impulsive behaviours and fluctuating moods are the dominant issues. Concerned adults seek clinical referral and adolescents' presentations commonly meet diagnostic criteria for attentional, behavioural and mood disorders. Diagnoses pertaining to attention and behaviour typically include Attention Deficit Hyperactivity Disorder (ADHD), Oppositional Defiant Disorder and Conduct Disorder. Mood disorders include Major Depressive Disorder, Bipolar Disorder and Disruptive Mood Dysregulation Disorder. Older adolescents and emerging adults who remain caught in limbic-stage configuration may receive diagnosis of Cluster B personality disorders, which are characterised by unpredictable and overly emotional thinking and behaviour, such as Borderline Personality Disorder, Histrionic Personality Disorder and Antisocial Personality Disorder. Following diagnosis, management of symptoms commonly includes medication.

Ongoing Implications

Any limbic-activated teenager will have a tendency to take risks, but entrenchment drives people beyond the margins of safety and integrity. These young people are prone to taking amplified risks and lack the cognitive features to apply self-control and prudent decision-making. Their developmental path is littered with provocative, oppositional and outrageous antics through which they very often cause harm to themselves and others. All too often impulsive behaviour leads to ongoing engagement with psychiatric services and/or the criminal justice system. Limbic dominance can leave these adolescents feeling very isolated and defective, with potentially lifelong struggles in relation to impulse control. This may show up in addictive personality traits, emotional volatility, aggression, unstable relationships, employment issues, criminal convictions and attunement difficulties when they become parents themselves.

Chapter 3

The Inhibitive Adolescent

Some young people progress through each of the three configuration styles in turn, starting off the teenage years as a relatively impulsive adolescent, then moving into the inhibitive stage of development before finally becoming directional. For these adolescents the configuration styles unfold in sequence. During the inhibitive years impulsive behaviours continue, to be sure, though are less figural than before. Adolescents become a little more narcissistic now – not in a pathological way, but in the spirit of self-development.

In order to have a strong sense of self, adolescents spend time getting to know who they are and wondering about how others think of them. This is the time when activity in the cerebral cortex is intensified, a brain area responsible for more sophisticated functioning such as reasonable, balanced decision-making and emotional containment. This part of the brain is also known as the seat of thinking and fires up when we are focusing, concentrating, figuring things out and paying attention. Whilst these adolescents engage in more thinking, not all elements of the cerebral cortex are fully matured and there is not yet optimal connectivity between its constituent parts. This work in progress translates as adolescents not quite having access to bigger-picture consideration, so their reflections tend to be overly self-involved as they struggle to see the wood for the trees. Hence thinking can be more self-absorbed than rational and with a tendency to be somewhat negative, particularly about themselves. The inhibitive stage of development is characterised by personal insecurity and self-consciousness which brings its own drama.

Adolescents who present with an inhibitive configuration style tend to internalise experience and assign personal significance to the most innocuous of situations. For example, Magda has wanted a particular pair of shoes for so long and takes ages deliberating over the colour to choose. When she finally purchases them, she wears them into town to meet her friends. Later that week a friend remarks to the group that whilst she likes this style of shoe, in her opinion, they make people's feet look big. Convinced that her classmate is having a dig at her, Magda vows never to wear the shoes again, comes home and throws them in the bin.

DOI: 10.4324/9781003373599-5

Sometime later, Magda orders a dress online for an upcoming night out. She tries it on, and it is perfect. The arrangement is that all the girls will get ready at Pamela's house, whose mum will then drop them at the disco. On Friday evening when she gets home from school, Magda packs her bag with the various necessities and tries on her dress again. This time she doesn't like how it sits on her – she looks fat and takes it off immediately. She is definitely not going to wear the dress and proceeds to try on outfit after outfit with increasing urgency and frustration. Her mother comes in to see what all the fuss is about and finds her daughter in a panic, giving out about how fat she is and announcing in high drama that she won't be going to the disco after all, as nothing fits her. By this time, virtually every stitch of clothing in her wardrobe has been tried on and consigned to the floor. Magda's mother tries to help, reassuring her about what a beautiful figure she has and suggesting she try the new dress again or maybe that gorgeous white one that she wore recently. Her mother's attempt to help only make the situation worse and Magda shouts at mum to get out and leave her alone. The adolescent flings herself on top of her bed and cries sorely. She sees herself through a negative lens, convinced of her unacceptability and preoccupied with what everyone at the disco will think of her. Magda imagines that her peers think as obsessively about her as she does, and the teenager feels truly wretched about herself and her life momentarily. However, after a brief exchange of social media messages with friends about her predicament, the adolescent's persecutory attitude ebbs. She feels reassured and cheered up. A short time later, Magda arrives in the kitchen and announces that she needs a lift over to Pamela's. The new dress is packed in her bag and she ends up having a great night. Despite Magda having created a mini tornado in the house, next day there isn't a word about the drama.

As the sense of self deepens, friendships and relationships may become more intense and invested. And whilst they are less reactive than impulsive teenagers, inhibitive adolescents have not yet reached maturity – emotional intensity features strongly, and wobbles are still the order of the day. As they develop a richer capacity to find language for their experience, so they are more able to put words to how they are feeling which can help if they are prone to drowning in the intensity of their inner worlds. With an inhibitive configuration style, Linda struggles to feel understood, resorting to songwriting and poetry to express her emotional intensity and burgeoning sense of existential isolation. She tells me that she creates some of her most profound work when she is drunk, though is frustrated when she wakens in the morning and can't read her own handwriting from the night before. Inhibitive adolescents are in touch both with their uniqueness and their wish to belong, which can feel confusing. Linda confides in me a yearning to be 'normal' which runs parallel to her deep fear of being 'ordinary'…there is a fine line between the two and the adolescent feels an urgency to get the right balance. Linda sobs heartfelt tears about her dilemma during several sessions. The fascination with the self manifests in a preoccupation with how others perceive her and gives rise to all kinds of uncertainty and insecurity before she eventually finds more solid ground. During this time of great tenderness, emotional intensity and self-consciousness, the adolescent is also developing increased independence, insight and psychological sophistication as adulthood emerges on the horizon. The next anticipated step for the inhibitive adolescent is to move into a more directional configuration style which ushers in stability, balance and greater self-assurance. However, as mentioned previously, plenty of adolescents do not progress sequentially through the three configuration styles. Many become entrenched in one or other as their development becomes fixed and stagnant. Let us explore the experience of entrenchment in the inhibitive configuration style.

Entrenched Inhibition

Whilst impulsivity wanes and gives way to a more inhibitive mode of being for a time, on the journey towards becoming directional adolescents, some young people bypass impulsivity altogether and do not experience the spontaneity and experimental spirit that some of their counterparts display. These cautious and tense adolescents demonstrate an entrenched inhibitive configuration style which defines their teenage journey and sense of self. Being inhibitive is not a developmental episode, but is a fixed experience through which all of their adolescence is filtered. In today's world we are seeing epidemic levels of teenagers living inhibitive lives to the extreme, who are highly self-critical, gripped by anxiety and struggling to attend school or even leave their bedrooms. These young people, in stark contrast to impulsive teenagers, tend not to live with spontaneity and feel easily overwhelmed. Where impulsive adolescents tend not to care much about their future or take life especially seriously, inhibitive teens approach life with the opposite mindset: they care too much and take things too seriously. Adolescents whose configuration style is extremely inhibitive typically bypass the impulsive stage of development almost entirely. Rather than not thinking about their actions, they consider and analyse everything, overthinking their way through the world and foregoing spontaneity. And with the lack of bigger-picture thinking, they are inclined towards negatively self-referenced thoughts…and lots of them. The outcome is often catastrophic thinking, where they worry and obsess about every possible negative outcome. Whereas their more impulsive peers are driven by pleasure and fun, inhibitive adolescents are in search of comfort. They seek experiences which neutralise anxiety and restore calm.

Brendan has always been mildly anxious, though this has escalated since starting secondary school and is increasingly impacting his and his entire family's life. He is plagued by intrusive thoughts which he finds very distressing. The principal focus of his negative obsession is his mother Hannah, who enjoys excellent health. He is unnecessarily and irrationally terrified and preoccupied that something bad is going to happen to her and no amount of reassurance on her part quells his anxiety. During the first week at his new school, Brendan calls and texts his mother relentlessly, double-checking that she is OK, reporting sore heads and tummy aches, pleading with her to come get him and becoming distraught when she refuses.

It has reached a point at home where Brendan follows Hannah everywhere. He accompanies her as she walks the dog, waits outside the bathroom (which remains unlocked at his insistence, in case she collapses and he needs to get in urgently) and sleeps on a mattress at the foot of her bed. The school has recently called the adolescent's mother to take him home as he was suffering from a panic attack after an ambulance drove past the school in the direction of their home. He was convinced it was for his mother. The teenager's anxiety levels are so high that the only way he manages to relieve his stress is to be in the physical presence of his mother. Life for Brendan has become about a moment-to-moment struggle to feel comfortable and calm.

The Inadequate Self

Inhibitive adolescents are driven by a pervasive sense of their own inadequacy and of not being good enough. Whilst we all hit into moments of this from time to time, these young people develop a relentless internal monologue of self-judgement, finding themselves lacking at every turn. Their hostile voice literally becomes their worst enemy as the reality of their experience is diminished with non-stop negative commentary directed towards themselves. Eventually it feels impossible for inhibitive adolescents to like themselves as this hostile voice almost takes on a life of its own. It is heart-breaking for parents to watch their wonderful, beautiful, kind, intelligent teenagers express nothing but contempt for themselves and spurn compliments or positive feedback.

Isabelle is fat, ugly and stupid. Her 'friends' aren't friends at all, they are just really nice girls who tolerate her but, in truth, they don't really want to be around her – even though they spend time with her in school and invite her to come places with them. She is such a burden to her parents that it is difficult for her to spend time with them. Mostly she just stays in her room, for when she is in their company, they inevitably ask her how she is doing, which is proof that they worry about her. This makes Isabelle deeply uncomfortable and the adolescent feels that if she wasn't there – sometimes physically present with them, and at other times, in the world at all – it would relieve her parents' worry and their lives would be better. Her parents are disappointed in her, she can see it in their eyes. Her only sanctuary is her bedroom, where she spends most of her time feeling bad about herself. This is also an important exam year for Isabelle, who finds it difficult to start studying as she is sure to fail everything and let everyone down – as usual.

In reality, Isabelle is a pleasant, gracious and attractive teen, who is a straight A student, too thin for her height and cherished by both her family and friends. Nevertheless, the hostile self-talk convinces her otherwise. This overshadows and dictates how she feels about herself, how she believes she is perceived by others, how she engages with the world and essentially her every waking moment. Inhibitive adolescents, like Isabelle, are often mentally drained by the relentless and uncompromising voice in their head. They also feel powerless to make it stop, which creates a sense of helplessness and despair.

Body Discomfort

Entrenched inhibitive adolescents tend to become negatively preoccupied with their bodies, focusing not on who they are, but on how they look. I cannot recall meeting a single adolescent who endured an entrenched inhibitive configuration style who felt comfortable with and in their body. Whilst it's typical for most adolescents to feel insecure about how they look, this intensely negative relationship with the body leaves inhibitive teenagers negatively focused on their appearance and can create considerable disgust and anxiety. Many view their bodies with contempt. In my practice, 'fat and ugly' are givens for most inhibitive adolescent girls I encounter. They endure endless self-shame because of their supposedly hideous bodies, whereas muscular physique and height tend to be the concerns for most of my male adolescent clients.

More recently I am meeting surging numbers of adolescents with entrenched inhibitive configuration style expressing gender dysphoria and, for whom, inhabiting their body creates profound distress. Orla is challenged by her parents when they discover that their daughter has been self-harming. With some relief and a lot of trepidation, the adolescent confides in their parents that they identify as transgender. Orla hates their girl's name and wants to be known as Luke and change pronouns. They tell their parents how they hate attending an all-girls school and dressing in a girl's uniform each day. Reluctantly, Luke's parents purchase a binder for them in exchange for Luke agreeing to refrain from cutting themselves. When we meet, the adolescent is frantic about starting puberty blockers and hormone therapy, feeling distraught at having to delay a double mastectomy due to their age, waiting lists and their parents' unwillingness to go privately. Our conversations alternate between descriptions of the extreme discomfort and suicidal feelings experienced in this alien body and the anticipated joy of full transition to being male. Luke's deep sense of discomfort and unease inhabiting their body is the overriding feature of their sense of self. The adolescent is convinced that the psychological discomfort they endure will evaporate when their physical discomfort is resolved.

In addition to negative body perception, the relationship to food is characteristically questionable and may be problematic for many inhibitive adolescents. An inflexible approach to their lifespace in general is also applied to eating. Restrictive calorie control and rigid eating practices are commonplace among this group who tend to overthink food, and whilst concerning, this doesn't necessarily merit diagnosis of an eating disorder. Natalie does not eat breakfast, has a plain chicken wrap for lunch and cooks the same evening meal – a vegetable stir fry – at the same time every day, weighing out the ingredients precisely. She waits until the other members of her family have finished their evening meal and exited the kitchen before preparing her food. Natalie also goes to the gym three days a week and goes for a run the other four. Exercise for the teenager modulates her guilt at eating food. The thought of taking a day off is unimaginable and the familiarity of this routine keeps

Natalie's anxiety and discomfort about being fat from reaching overwhelming levels. The adolescent's relationship with body, food and exercise merits an anorectic profile and is several degrees away from full-blown anorexia – like so many other inhibitive teenage girls I meet, who remain subclinical. Some go on to receive diagnosis of an anorexic eating disorder. Whilst impulsive teens tend to eat for pleasure, it would seem that inhibitive adolescents tend to do precisely the opposite – their comfort is derived from *not* eating.

Exercise and a strict dietary programme are the order of the day for sixteen-year-old James, who is intent on bulking up by eating a minimum of 3000 calories per day. He hates how skinny and gangly he looks and is determined to develop a strong, ripped physique. He tells me that he wants chest and arm muscles that bulge when he wears short-sleeved button-up shirts, so that it seems as though he is bursting out of his clothes. Protein is the holy grail and he eats steak for breakfast before school, whether he feels like it or not. Mostly he doesn't feel like eating it, but inhibitive adolescents tend to be extremely disciplined – overriding their impulses and doing what *should* be done as opposed to doing what they *feel* like doing. In addition, he spends hours planning and undertaking weights workouts in his garage in order to strengthen and sculpt his body into a more acceptable frame. James also plays Gaelic football and takes his training and matches extremely seriously. He has a tendency to overpractice and ignore injuries. His intense nature means that he feels very anxious before matches and, as well as being highly competitive, he can't handle his team losing. After games where he doesn't play especially well, he descends into a particularly foul mood and spends hours and days forensically scrutinising his every move on the pitch, berating himself for his performance. James is devastated when his manager explains that he hasn't been selected for the under-eighteen county panel because he does not have the right mindset. This bewilders the adolescent who knows he is one of their best players and feels that he never gives less than one hundred per cent commitment to his club. James cannot see that his intensity and insecurity are the issue.

Probably most young people experience episodes of body insecurity and become self-conscious about their appearance during the course of adolescence or even during the course of every day, shuttling between complaining about being fat and eating pizza and chocolate. However, those who are staunchly inhibitive take this to more extreme levels. Their caustic thoughts translate into rigid, punishing regimes as they attempt to compensate for inadequacy and feelings of unacceptability. On the other hand, whilst exercise is important to and even obsessive for many adolescents like Isabelle and James, there are plenty of inhibitive adolescents who are exercise phobic too. For example, Leanne's passion is all things anime and manga – either creating artwork or watching animations all day long. She hates being outside or doing exercise. During the pandemic, her parents made Leanne and her siblings spend time in the garden every day during the fine weather. The adolescent stood uncomfortably on a spot in the garden with her hands in her pockets until it was time to go back indoors. She does whatever she can to avoid sports at school, including asking her parents to write notes, feigning period pains, forging notes and forgetting her kit. One morning, when her dad refused to write her a note, she threatened to call social services and report him for violating her human rights.

School as a Pressure Chamber

A tragic reality for most adolescents who demonstrate a fixed inhibitive configuration style is that, irrespective of their talents and abilities, they tend not to have much, if any, faith in themselves. Their keen sense of not being good enough underscores most dimensions of their lifespace as they pursue the myth that if they appear outwardly acceptable, then this will create an internal sense of validation: *If I am deemed acceptable in the eyes of others, then maybe I'll start to feel acceptable to myself.* This sets the scene for perfectionism as adolescents put themselves under enormous pressure in order to achieve an acceptable status. The end result is often great outward success coupled with continuing feelings of low self-worth, creating a dual reality of appearing to have it made but feeling miserable inside. Nowhere is this more apparent than in relation to academic work.

As students, these adolescents who endure entrenched inhibitive configuration styles have massive academic expectations for themselves and project these expectations on to relevant adults also. They are highflyers and push to be the best whilst feeling obligated not to disappoint parents and teachers. That's quite a burden of responsibility for young shoulders to carry. And because our society values education so highly, their assumptions about who they are and how they become acceptable are endorsed when high grades are celebrated, and praise is heaped on teenagers. The pressure appears worth it for a top grade.

Whilst achievement doesn't shift the feelings of not being good enough, it does garner a level of external acceptability. And so, a cycle begins of excessive effort leading to achievement, which brings interpersonal recognition together with a gnawing emptiness inside. This externalised sense of self is an all-too-common experience for adolescents who experience school as an unrelenting pressure chamber, as the quest for perfection and acceptability moves to unsustainable levels.

Daisy takes her studies very seriously and worries a lot about school and her future. A perfectionist, she often overstudies for homework and exams, foregoing sleep as she regularly works on projects until well after midnight. Her efforts are constantly undermined by the 'not-good-enough' voice in her head which drives her to double down and work even harder. Daisy is an A student across the board, top in her class in most subjects. When her chemistry teacher announces a class test for the following Friday, the adolescent feels the familiar wave of anxiety rising through her. A rational response might be:

'I'm sitting comfortably in this subject and understand the topic I'm being questioned on. All I need to do is a few hours of study to ensure I do well. Worst case scenario, I do nothing, and I'll still ace it. Besides, it's just a class test and

doesn't count towards my Leaving Cert grade. I can have a life and still do well in this test.'

However, neurotic anxiety takes hold and she goes into a spin. A lack of faith in herself means that the test takes on a life-or-death importance and the more anxious she feels, the more time she spends studying. Unable to sleep, eat or think about anything else, Daisy's anxiety threatens to undermine her academic performance. Despite knowing her topic well, she feels desperately underprepared. On the morning of the exam, she feels sick to her stomach, has a panic attack and requires colossal support and encouragement from parents to get in through the doors of the school. The exam consists of twenty questions, of which Daisy knows that she answered nineteen correctly. She makes a decent attempt at the last one but isn't confident with her answer. Approaching the situation from a balanced perspective, she would understand that she has definitely passed well and perhaps would feel mild irritation with the one she didn't get fully correct. However, perfectionists don't settle for good enough and Daisy obsesses about the test for the next week, convincing herself that she has failed the entire paper, until her chemistry teacher releases the class grades. She receives ninety-five per cent and feels more frustrated than satisfied with her result, unable to forgive herself for losing those few marks.

Chapter 4

The Anxious Lifespace

The most pervasive struggle for adolescents who demonstrate an entrenched inhibitive configuration style is *anxiety*. Of course, impulsive adolescents and those inhibitive teens who are progressing sequentially through the three configuration styles experience anxiety at times. However, what sets the entrenched inhibitive configuration style apart is how pervasive and annihilating the experience is for these adolescents. In response to anxiety, their lifespace becomes defined by a need for comfort as they become invested in avoiding potentially anxious situations, sometimes at all costs. Entrenchment typically reduces the inhibitive adolescent's world to three dimensions of experience: a lifespace largely populated with threatening and dread-inducing people and situations; a small comfort zone which offers some degree of relief and breathing space; and a cluster of anxiety symptoms which act as a protective barrier to the comfort zone (Figure 4.1).

Often the anxious lifespace emerges in childhood and is well established by the adolescent years. Commonly, a parent is recruited into the comfort zone, on whom the child becomes very dependent. The presence of this comforting parent is a soothing balm for the uneasiness and fear that characterises the child's world. When other children are learning to become independent, inhibitive children are leaning heavily into adults with whom they feel safe. This can morph into a yearning to always be with the comforting parent. Feelings of dread and fear emerge when mum pops out to the shop or goes to the bathroom. Bedtimes are usually an ordeal.

Six-year-old Mia was an anxious child who was frightened of the dark, of spiders crawling over her bed, of ghosts and of burglars coming into her home – all of which diminished when she was in the presence of a comfort parent. Her mother Elisa spent ages each night reassuring her daughter that she was safe and that nothing bad was going to happen. Mia insisted that her mother stay with her until she fell asleep, so Elisa would have to spend up to an hour lying beside her daughter. Whilst this was a tiresome rigmarole, Elisa also experienced it as an important bonding time for the pair, as this was when her daughter opened up and shared all her worries. Predictably, Elisa was wakened later each night by Mia standing by her parents' bedside because she couldn't sleep. Mia offered various reasons for this including nightmares, sore tummies, hearing burglars, a hole in her back and

DOI: 10.4324/9781003373599-6

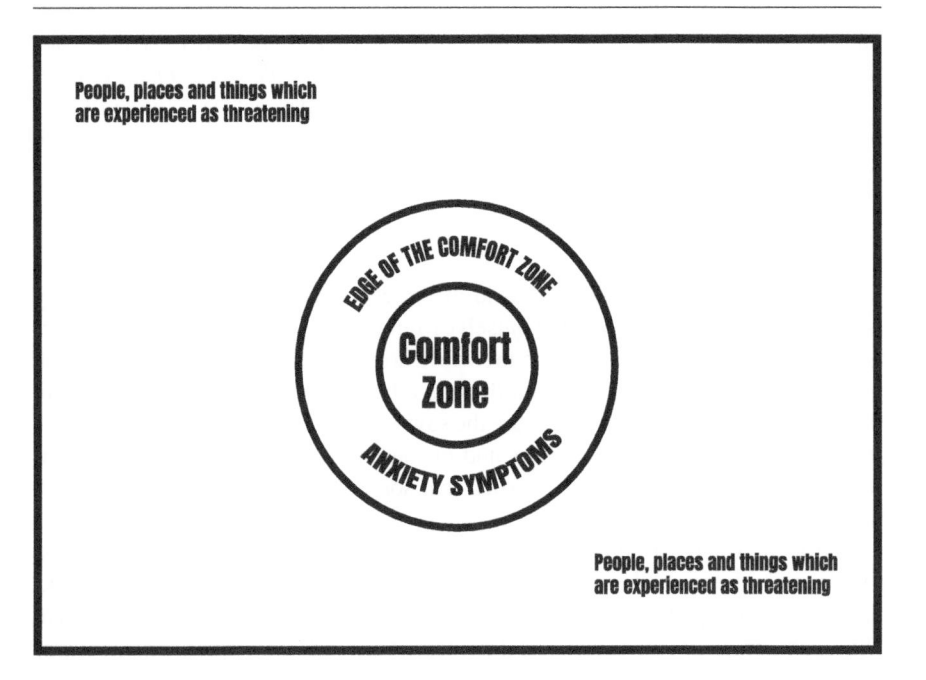

People, places and things which
are experienced as threatening

EDGE OF THE COMFORT ZONE

Comfort Zone

ANXIETY SYMPTOMS

People, places and things which
are experienced as threatening

Figure 4.1 The Anxious Lifespace

that her teddies were coming alive. She would then spend the remainder of the night sleeping comfortably and soundly with mum, the comfort parent, whilst dad was relegated to Mia's pink princess bed. As a teenager, Mia continues to battle with insomnia. She struggles to switch off from overthinking, though her rumination about ghosts and burglars have been replaced by forensic analysis of her day and the stresses of her academic workload.

Comfort zones for adolescents are restricted lifespaces – physically, emotionally, cognitively and interpersonally. Quite often, the inhibitive adolescents I meet feel comfortable only at home, and specifically, maybe only in their bedrooms. And whilst they certainly are sensitive, even hypersensitive, their emotional worlds can be limited to anxiety-related feelings such as dread, guilt, regret, sadness and worry. Responding to their world with joy, excitement, delight and contentment seem beyond their repertoire most of the time. Anxiety has a way of keeping adolescents flat inside too. Inhibitive adolescents' thoughts tend to be shaped by anxiety and filtered through the negative, self-deprecating lens of a still-developing cerebral cortex; whose connectivity does not yet include the psychological features which will support more reality-based, balanced perception. Guilt too, becomes an unwelcome guest in their minds and takes the good out of most situations and experiences. Always judging their own performance, particularly against others, inhibitive teens engage with peers through comparison and with a strong competitive edge: *I'm not pretty enough. She's thinner than me. I'm not smart enough. They think I'm stupid. I must score better than them. I'm not talented enough.* Forever seeking to improve in order to feel acceptable, these adolescents lack the self-belief and self-assurance which enables their more balanced counterparts to engage with greater confidence.

Friendship Triangles

Sometimes the comfort zone is devoid of direct human contact for very socially isolated adolescents who keep themselves removed even from family members and whose principal interactions in the world are online. Usually, however, at least one parent is recruited in and often there is a best friend or a group of friends in the comfort zone also. Friendships are the saving grace for many anxious teenagers who draw courage from their peers and manage to enjoy a social life. However, their propensity for dependency is such that some friendships have a tendency to end in failure and rejection.

Fourteen-year-old Jill has an entrenched inhibitive configuration style. She and Olivia are in the same class and are best friends. They spend time together at weekends and regularly sleep over at each other's houses. Jill's mother takes the girls to shows and organises other wonderful treats. Jill is a very considerate and generous friend – baking cupcakes for Olivia, giving her gifts and sending warm, caring messages. She trusts Olivia and feels that she could talk about anything to her. Jill arranges for them to meet up each morning before school so that they can walk in together. She makes sure that the girls sit beside each other in their lessons and misses her friend when classes are split. Science is one such subject where students are divided into classes within the whole year group, determined by their abilities. Olivia is doing foundation level GCSE science and finds herself in a class with Rebecca. The two girls share a desk and start to become friendly. Jill, however, is moved into higher tier science and dreads the thought of being separated from her best friend.

Previously having loved science, Jill endures the classes and is relieved to join her friend again when the bell rings. Olivia fill Jill in on any news or fun from science class and Rebecca's name is introduced into their conversation with increasing frequency. Olivia is in Jill's comfort zone and it is sealed closed – she has no interest in opening up the space for anyone else. So, rather than respond with interest and curiosity about this new girl, Jill experiences Olivia's science class pal as a threat to their friendship. The adolescent's narrative becomes *Rebecca is trying to take Olivia away from me.*

Sometime later, as Olivia is preparing to celebrate her birthday, she decides to have a party and sleepover for her friends. The formerly perfect friendship – almost too good to be true, with so much giving and thoughtful consideration from Jill – starts to unravel. Olivia experiences a dilemma: she definitely wants her new friend there because the two girls get on really well and have so much fun together. Ideally, also, she would like to invite Jill. However, she knows that Jill will be insulted and will huff if this new girl joins the party – the adolescent has begun to feel smothered and controlled by Jill. Olivia's hunch is that if she were to invite Jill to the party, she would feel under duress to sit beside her all night and make sure that she is OK. She starts to feel the burden of being in a friendship with a dependent peer, and without conscious awareness of the process, prefers the freedom and mutuality she feels when she is with Rebecca, her new friend. Jill is high maintenance and inviting her to the party means that there will be tensions: Olivia will feel responsible for her and the night might be soured. Jill's absence would guarantee a great sleepover, and so, with some mild guilt, Olivia decides against inviting her.

A few weeks later Jill hears mention of the party. By this time, her resentment is growing, and she is struggling a lot with how the new girl is coming in between her and her best friend. Olivia seems to be forgetting about her and being excluded from the birthday party is the final straw. Jill is devastated – how could her friend treat her like this, after all she did for her? The adolescent's narrative shifts to *those two girls are bullying me.*

Jill's mother attempts to sort the friendship drama out between the parents and when this backfires, approaches the principal as her daughter is distraught and now having panic attacks on school mornings. Appalled at how Jill is being treated and how the school is doing nothing about it, she persists. The school responds by having the form teacher talk to Olivia and Rebecca about the importance of being kind and treating others with respect. Jill is invited to join the meeting after some time and the other two girls are asked to apologise to her. Olivia and Rebecca have been labelled as bullies and feel harassed by the level of adult involvement.

According to Jill and her mother, this whole episode is all down to Rebecca's blatant and artful manipulation, as she wilfully set out to ruin the original friendship. However, the dependency and passivity of Jill's entrenched inhibitive configuration style, and how this showed up in her friendship with Olivia, is the fundamental issue. Olivia was put in the impossible situation of being the connector in their friendship triangle – friend to both though unable to enjoy three-way collaboration – a common phenomenon between adolescent girls where at least one member of the triad is strongly inhibitive. Jill's insecurity and lack of mutuality in her contact became more and more unappealing, heralding the end of the friendship.

A similar experience had happened to Jill in primary school after which she had felt forced to move to a new school. The family were considering a similar move now as she was wholly socially isolated. In each instance, Jill had put all of her eggs in one basket, so to speak, and leaned heavily on a single friend for emotional and social support. Each time a friendship buckled under the weight of Jill's dependency, she had no backup and faced social isolation once more.

Edge of the Comfort Zone

As inhibitive adolescents tend to become invested in avoiding anxiety-provoking experience, the lifespace becomes organised in a manner which differentiates what is comfortable from what is not. People and situations which don't make them feel comfortable don't make it into the comfort zone and are experienced as threats. School is an example of this – with its dual challenges of academic pressure and navigating the interpersonal world of fellow students and teachers. It is unusual for me to meet an adolescent who demonstrates an entrenched inhibitive configuration style who loves school. It's often important to them, but many find it difficult to tolerate the stress of being there. Attendance records are questionable for some who struggle to make it in every day, whilst others feel so overwhelmed, they cannot cope with attending at all.

Entrenched inhibitive teenagers are almost the reverse of impulsive adolescents and their spontaneous, laid-back, cavalier attitude to life. Changes to routine and new experiences can be angst-inducing and may upset the balance of familiarity and relative relief found within the comfort zone. This creates a lot of stress for adolescents who find it difficult to embrace the flow of life with its constant shifting and uncertainty. Inhibitive adolescents overthink their way through the teenage years neurotically analysing, rehashing and second-guessing situations – and stressing themselves out immensely in the process. Anything which threatens the integrity of the comfort zone is to be dreaded. In fact, much of their headspace is taken up with worrying about what *could* happen. I refer to this as *the-thought-of-it-itis* where adolescents are unnerved and even terrorised by the *thought* of things going wrong. They freak out a little, or a lot, at the thought of going to school, the thought of being in a group of people, the thought of failing exams, the thought of leaving home to go to college, the thought of mum dying, the thought of them dying, the thought of exams, the thought of going into the shop to buy a bar of chocolate. It is at this point that symptoms emerge as negative thoughts create anxious feelings: panic attacks, tears, phobias, OCD, tummy aches, dizziness, tics and paralysing fear which prevents them from going to school or engaging in other activities and events are just some of the many expressions of their anxiety. This cycle perpetuates itself and spins out of control as anxious feelings now give rise to even more negative thoughts which generate increased anxiety, and so on. Some adolescents spend much of their waking hours in this negative feedback loop of overthinking and feeling anxious.

The Anxious Body

When someone perceives a threat, the body reacts by becoming hyperaroused and secreting stress hormones including cortisol and adrenaline as the system prepares for self-preservation through fight, flight or freeze. Once the threat has passed the body returns to its natural, more relaxed state. For example, if someone hears a loud unexpected noise in their home, in an instant, stress hormones will typically surge through their system. Their brain and body will brace for danger. What is this threat? The possibility of an intruder or some other danger flashes into their thoughts as they are momentarily gripped with terror. Then they hear the dog scuttling around and realise he's knocked over the ironing board. All is well again – stress hormones are called off and the person's sense of balance and safety is restored once more.

Entrenched inhibitive adolescents inhabit threatening lifespaces, fearful of so many bad things happening, troubled by how they have messed up and feeling panicky about how they'll not be able to handle future situations. As they focus their attention for hours at a time on what did or could go wrong, they become worked up, endlessly stressing themselves out. Their systems are saturated with stress hormones which can overactivate the immune system and trigger inflammation. In my clinical practice over the years I have noted patterns in how stress maps on to the body in chronically anxious adolescents. Bearing in mind that I'm not medically trained…when I enquire about the adolescent's general health, there seem to be four main areas of the body which are targeted by this persistent activation of the stress response system. Here are some of the most common complaints described to me by adolescents and their parents:

Gastrointestinal tract: tummy aches, nausea, irritable bowel syndrome, constipation, diarrhoea, food allergies, colitis and Crohn's disease.

Chest: tightness, heaviness or pain in the chest, palpitations, asthma, shortness of breath, feeling unable to take a deep breath, or feeling breathless and feeling constricted in the throat.

Skin: eczema, psoriasis, shingles, acne, rashes, itching and very sensitive skin.

Head: headaches, sinus problems, insomnia, dizziness, fainting, blurred vision and tingling sensations.

For inhibitive adolescents, an enduring stress response is created. Overthinking, which tends to principally focus on threat and inadequacy, reverberates in the body. As young people live in fear and convince themselves of their deep lack of worth, their bodies remain in a never-ending cycle of physiological arousal. Much of the lifespace engenders intense discomfort and parents look on powerlessly as this oppressive experience overtakes their teenager's world.

Anxiety Meltdowns

As inhibitive adolescents reach the edge of their comfort zones and threat feels more tangible, a part of the limbic system known as the amygdala can become activated. This is triggered when we perceive that our safety and even our very survival is at stake. It is a transmarginal stress response which sends the adolescent into extreme panic, resulting in various types of meltdown including tearful collapses, rage attacks and numbing out. On the first morning of each new academic term many inhibitive adolescents become amygdalated knowing that they have to face another term of academic pressure and social unease. The stress from being out of their comfort zone is a grim reality staring them in the face – no longer on the horizon but happening right now. The thought of putting on the dreaded uniform and walking through the front door of the school building – and having to do it repeatedly until the next school break – pushes many over the edge.

Paula tends to freeze when her amygdala starts overfiring. As a younger child she felt unable to move and get out of her bed on school mornings. Her parents would take turns dressing her as she sat on their knee motionless. Her father describes the experience akin to dressing a rag doll. As an adolescent Paula manages to dress herself on school mornings but remains expressionless and muted around home and on the school run. When they reach the school gates, Paula sometimes feels paralysed in the passenger seat of the car, unable to move or speak. After reassurance and encouragement has come to nothing, the parents drive her home and hope for a better outcome the following day.

Similarly, Amanda was prone to worrying and feeling anxious even as a child. Despite attending school, playing football, going to dance class and having playmates, she struggled with taking life too seriously and had little confidence. Transition to secondary school was a challenge for her at first, though when she grew familiar with the new environment and made a new friend, it felt slightly more manageable.

Although highly intelligent, Amanda worries about not being a good enough student and spends a lot of time on homework. On school mornings, she feels weak and nauseous, offloading her fears and anxieties on her mother, whose reassurances don't seem to help. Whilst very sensible and mature, the adolescent is emotionally much younger than her peers. She has never been to a disco and prefers to spend Friday nights with family. Discos are noisy and full of drunken teens, why would she want to go there? During summer term, her whole class is invited to an overnight camping party, though Amanda chooses to stay at her aunt's house that night as her twin cousins are turning six and the family is renting a bouncy castle. She finds growing up difficult and threatening and would have loved to have remained longer in primary school. Adulthood scares her.

Amanda has also developed health issues related to her anxiety over the years. She is plagued with digestive issues, eczema and asthma which all seem to worsen with elevated stress levels. Amanda opts for a vegan diet and is preoccupied with her weight. She completes 200 crunches each morning before school, uses her dad's home gym in the evenings and restricts her calorie intake. Despite all her effort, Amanda misguidedly continues to perceive herself as being overweight, hating her big tummy and how fat her thighs are. As the COVID-19 pandemic unfolds and people are instructed to stay at home, Amanda remains in her comfort zone. She lives mostly in her bedroom with her dog as company, spending a vast amount of time on screens. Amanda loves that her family are all at home and that she doesn't have to go to school. Whilst she worries somewhat about loved ones dying from the virus, overall, she feels very safe and comfortable during this extended period of time spent in lockdown. Amanda's comfort zone becomes an increasingly reassuring space as days and weeks turn into months. Her anxiety levels have never been so low.

Figure 4.2 Amanda's Anxious Lifespace

As restrictions lift and schools reopen, Amanda struggles with resuming regular life and stepping out of her comfort zone (Figure 4.2). A consequence of the adolescent's extended time being insulated from regular life is that the limited capacity she had possessed for navigating an anxiety-provoking world prior to the pandemic has now been lost. She experiences a tsunami of anxiety at the thought of being out in the world again, refusing to resume football and dancing. Returning to school feels like an impossible task for the adolescent and she becomes extremely upset at even the idea of going to school. Amygdala hijack means that her attempts to go into school are often aborted and, on the days she manages to attend, Amanda struggles to stay in school for the entire day. Before long, she is absent more days than she is present and has begun to study only when absolutely necessary, as this brings school to mind. By the time I meet Amanda she is phobic both about academic work and school attendance.

Unfortunately for Amanda, the landscape of peer connections has transformed during lockdown too and she is no longer part of the friendship group she had once belonged to. The adolescent spends hours on her phone comparing herself to other girls and feeling miserable seeing their fabulous figures and wonderful social lives, while she is a fat, ugly, pathetic mess who just stays in her room and has no life. She wishes she could feel normal and not have to overthink everything or agonise over every minute decision. The adolescent finds it so difficult and frustrating to even form an opinion on something – her frame of reference is always what others would think. Amanda tries hard to be positive on the outside when she is at school, but inside she is gripped with anxiety and second-guesses every nuance of interaction.

Amanda also had trouble falling asleep at night. Compulsive bedtime rituals stop helping as she remains unable to switch off from her forensic analysis of life – wondering what she could have said or done to make her friends not like her, microscopically reviewing her day and berating herself for being such a loser. Cutting herself becomes a strategy for momentarily stopping the overthinking and hostile self-narrative. Amanda is perpetually annoyed at herself and feels frozen in her comfort zone, lacking the courage to push beyond it. She is daunted by the threat of life beyond its boundary yet feels miserable that life is passing her by. She feels utterly stuck. This intolerable experience of overthinking, horrible anxiety symptoms and not having the freedom to live the life she wants leaves the adolescent feeling mentally shattered. She appears depressed and whilst she isn't suicidal, it remains an option on the table and one she thinks about every day.

Intensity and Agitation

Adolescent anxiety, in general, tends to be easily recognisable primarily due to the presence of visual clues we associate with it such as panic attacks, nervous stomachs and tears, as well as the young person's willingness to offer a description of their experience. This collapse response lays bare the adolescent's discomfort and vulnerability. However, other adolescents are inclined to circumvent their anxious feelings and present as touchy and ill-tempered, in a waspish or abusive manner – which gets expressed particularly to those closest to them. Anxiety can be more difficult to spot in these teenagers and is often mistaken for arrogance or anger. These young people tend to be intense and edgy, and they are invested in defending themselves against feeling or being perceived as anxious or vulnerable.

Gary is one such adolescent. He spends a good deal of time overthinking and comparing himself to other peers. He wants to study medicine at college and puts pressure on himself to achieve top grades. His response to stressful and anxiety-provoking situations is to become frustrated and uptight, working himself into a bad mood. His hair not sitting right in the morning before school is enough to cause irritation and leave him feeling off-balance for the rest of the day. Exposing each other's weak spots in a way teenagers are especially artful at doing, some impulsive classmates hone in on Gary's intensity. They intuitively recognise that he takes himself too seriously and taunt him about girls, being gay, being attracted to teachers, being thin, being smart, his hair, the way he walks and generally annoy him through humour whenever an opportune moment arises. During these moments, the blood rushes to Gary's face as he flushes with embarrassment. His impulsive peers find this visible reaction hilarious. When he defends himself, this gives rise to even more jibing. Gary holds his anxiety and discomfort internally during the day, becoming wound up like a coiled spring in the process. In the evenings he comes home in a foul mood and take his frustration out on parents and siblings in a hostile and sometimes intimidating manner. Gary doesn't often feel at ease and as a result, family members' experience of living with him range from unpleasant to grim.

Gary's mother picks him and his sister Emma up from school each afternoon and is able to identify by the way her son walks to the car whether or not this will be a good evening. Sometimes, if she engages with him at all on the drive home, he can be particularly rude and ill-tempered. At home, the adolescent seems determined to provoke conflict with his parents, which tends to happen when his anxiety levels have escalated. This is in sharp contrast to his sibling's demeanour when she feels the same. On mornings when his mother is late leaving the house to drop Gary and his sister off to school, Emma invariably gets herself into an anxious spin – worrying about having to walk into class late, teachers being cross, being marked absent and what other students will think of her. She becomes tearful and pleads with her mother to stay home for the day. Gary, on the other hand, swears and shouts at his mother telling her what a useless driver and fucking idiot she is, kicking the back of the driver's seat as he verbally attacks her. Both teenagers were equally stressed and anxious about being late for school, though each expressed this in a very different manner. Gary's parents bring him to see me because of his anger management issues and their reluctance to continue treading on eggshells around their son. However, unknown to all of them, including Gary, anxiety is at the heart of his intense and disagreeable demeanour. At an opportune moment, as I tentatively suggest to Gary that he is filled with anxiety, he nods and becomes tearful with the relief of being seen and understood by us both.

Where other adolescents may endure persistently negative thoughts and debilitating symptoms which engender vulnerable feelings, young people who struggle with an entrenched inhibitive configuration style and who hold their anxiety in more intense and aggressive ways follow a predictable anxiety loop (Figure 4.3). From a relatively calm space, an important event or perhaps a buildup of anxious thoughts and minor situations triggers stressful feelings. These adolescents become saturated with overthinking, feelings of inadequacy and pressure. Attempts to repress this stress vary in success and usually at home, or on the sports field, it gets expressed as agitation. And whilst others will descend into a panic attack, these teenagers are more likely to become combative and offensive, offloading their stress in sometimes threatening and vicious ways. Parents and siblings tend to be common targets. Once anxiety and stress levels have been reduced, young people commonly express sorrow and regret for the things they have said and the hurt they have caused – leading to forgiveness, reassurance and the reinstating of calm…until next time.

Alex spends much of their time on screens in their room. They appreciate the relative comfort of a restricted lifespace, but also struggle with overthinking, gender dysphoria, social isolation and school-life pressure. When anxiety levels leave them feeling under threat, Alex grows stressed and becomes very tense. They rant to parents about the untidy house and quarrel about the simplest of things, such as not being able to find their favourite socks, storming off and slamming doors.

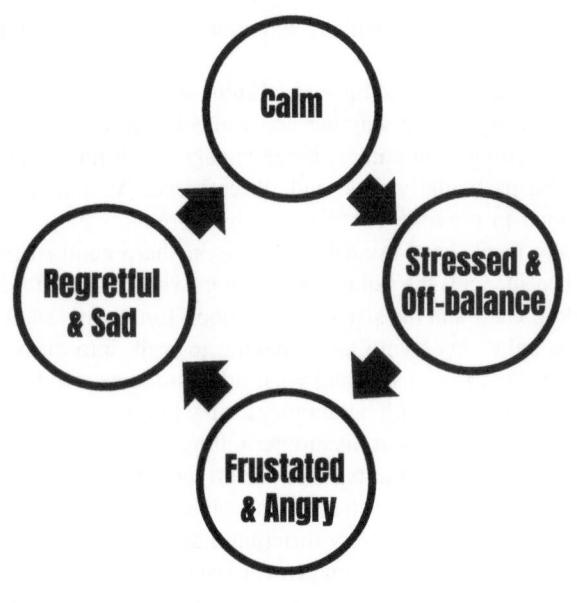

Figure 4.3 The Frustration Cycle

The adolescent declares their contempt for parents, chastises their mother for being obese and makes statements about wishing they were never born. Afterwards, Alex breathes easier and feels calmer. Apologies are made and hugs are exchanged as equilibrium is momentarily restored.

Diagnosis

When the cerebral cortex is still developing and the process of connecting the various parts of the brain together is not yet fully complete, intensity, anxiety and negatively coloured thinking can be the result. A lack of courage and little faith in themselves turns the relatively innocuous stresses of teenage life into monumental challenges. As rigidity and restriction begin to impact the young person's day-to-day functioning in the world, psychological assessment may be considered. Diagnoses pertaining to anxiety and overthinking include Generalised Anxiety Disorder, Panic Disorder, Obsessive Compulsive Disorder and Autism Spectrum Disorder. Older adolescents and emerging adults who persistently demonstrate an overly cognitive and anxious approach to the lifespace may receive diagnosis of Cluster A personality disorders such as Paranoid Personality Disorder, Schizoid Personality Disorder and Schizotypal Personality Disorder. In some cases, adolescents may go on to receive a diagnosis of Schizophrenia.

At twelve years of age Gareth received a diagnosis of Autism Spectrum Disorder. They are academically a high achiever, ace exams and have great belief in their intellectual prowess, to the point of being arrogant. Their principal identity marker is their intelligence – Gareth is the really smart kid and a walking encyclopaedia of facts about all manner of things. Despite this capacity, the adolescent struggles with many other dimensions of their experience. Social interaction and emotional overwhelm continue to be problematic and they experience a great deal of anxiety and time spent overthinking. School is a place of discomfort and they long for the day they can leave. Gareth also identifies as non-binary and yearns for the freedom of college where they can finally give expression to who they truly are. Gareth can't wait to get away. Their parents don't understand, and they hate living in small-town Ireland with its prejudice and parochial mindset. The adolescent takes offence at being known as 'the quirked up white boy' by peers. The adolescent's biggest dilemma, however, is how profoundly they hate themselves: they are an ugly, disgusting, pathetic excuse for a human being. Everything about them is defective.

Gareth has their sights firmly set on gaining a place at a prestigious university to study physics and willingly accepts their place on the course. Whilst academically more than capable of their study programme, the adolescent becomes gripped with anxiety about their new world. The adolescent finds it difficult to speak to people, struggles to attend lectures and fails to hand in assignments. Gareth does not possess the emotional, social and administrative skills to navigate college life and eventually has to confess the unmanageability of student life to his parents. They are utterly out of their comfort zone and drowning in overwhelm. Gareth takes a year out, tries again the following year and the year after, each time ending in collapse, disappointment and returning home. Living with such intense self-contempt and its cascade effects of social unease and anxious preoccupation make expanding their lifespace almost impossible for Gareth. In the end, they find an IT job within a local business and settle there temporarily, feeling crestfallen and humiliated. It is at this point that I meet the adolescent. Therapy becomes a lifeline for them as Gareth embarks on the process of making meaning of their experience, expanding their comfort zone and extending their repertoire of personal and relational skills.

Chapter 5

The Directional Adolescent

For many adolescents, towards the latter years of adolescence, the frontal lobe in the cerebral cortex comes online in a more pronounced manner and acts like a sort of mission control, linking all of the brain systems together. Until now the adolescent's self-experience has been principally organised in the limbic system and the not fully matured cerebral cortex. These young people moving sequentially through configuration styles continue to cycle through impulsive and inhibitive episodes to be sure, though with less intensity now. We begin to see more mature functioning and catch glimpses of an emerging adult. Greater frontal lobe activation introduces new capacities into the young person's repertoire of functioning. It exerts its influence on limbic activity and we see more self-discipline, choicefulness and resilience in adolescents at this stage. Connectivity of the frontal lobe supports the possibility of greater balance – emotionally, cognitively, socially and existentially. Impulses can be more easily contained, and the self-referenced ruminating of inhibitive experience gives way to a more measured perception. Directional adolescents have their act together. They tend to have a fair idea of what they want and move towards their objectives. We witness them discerning what's best for them and carrying through on their intentions with personal conviction and relative self-mastery.

The adolescent is no longer at the mercy of their impulses nor fettered by self-conscious preoccupation. Feeling good and belonging still feature, for sure, though they are now tempered by more sophisticated considerations with the development of a stronger sense of personal accountability. The intensity and neurotic presentation of the inhibitive configuration style is replaced by higher-level thinking and equanimity. A greater degree of freedom and innate resilience emerge as the young person shifts from an externally referenced to a self-directed approach to life. As the systems in the adolescent brain integrate and move in the direction of optimal connectivity between the parts, young people become increasingly in touch with a solid sense of reality, demonstrating self-control and mental flexibility. Functions such as decision-making and planning, which were previously influenced by what the adolescent felt like doing or by negatively self-referenced overthinking, are now characterised by considered reflection, greater balance, composure and even-temperedness.

DOI: 10.4324/9781003373599-7

The allure of temptation and risk-taking which arises in the limbic system continues. However, adolescents can now apply bigger-picture thinking and can realistically consider the implications of their actions. For example, Ciaran has an important college exam on Monday morning. His friends are having a party on Saturday and he really feels like going. He would love to chill out all weekend, get drunk and have fun – that's what he *feels* like doing. And he certainly doesn't feel like spending the weekend revising. A few years back, when the adolescent was fifteen and still limbic-activated, he would have been very invested in doing just this and would have tried hard to convince his parents to let him attend the party, spinning all manner of tall yarns or figuring ways to sneak out without getting caught – anything to avoid boring, pointless study. However, Ciaran's frontal lobe now participates in this process, enabling him to override his impulse to party and to avoid the tedium of preparing for his exam. He has now developed the capacity to apply containment and discipline to limbic activity. As Ciaran widens his decision-making lens, what feels good is overruled by what he deems is the right thing to do. He figures out that whilst he'll have a great time at the party, it'll be a late night and he'll be nursing a hangover the following day which will essentially cancel out any study plans for the weekend. The adolescent doesn't want to have to repeat this module, because that would complicate his final year of college. As his moral development is more advanced, he also reflects on the wider implications of any potential actions. Ciaran also takes into consideration the fact that his parents are paying his tuition fees and living expenses. He knows that extending his time at university will have financial implications for them. Despite his urge to socialise, the adolescent declines his friends' invitation and spends most of the weekend at his desk. Ciaran has developed discipline over his emotional arousal, so that he isn't exclusively driven by feeling good and peer belonging any longer. Frontal lobe activity creates a sense of composure and self-possession in response to the emergence of impulses and urges. Where the adolescent previously reacted to experiences and situations, he now demonstrates an ability to be choiceful. For directional adolescents, the future starts to come into view, and they are much less inclined to dismiss the unfolding significance of their actions for momentary feel-good.

Frontal lobe activity powerfully modulates the experience of anxiety and diffuses rigidly obsessive, self-denigrating perception which tends to feature for the more inhibitive adolescent. Adolescents step back from the confinement of negative feedback loops and balance the tendency to overthink with greater capacity to consider alternative interpretations of experience. Increased sophistication in the way of thinking about the self and one's place in the world generates greater freedom. Self-obsession is replaced by a new conceptual self-awareness as frontal lobe activity equips the young person to develop greater accuracy and less neurotic bias in discerning their identity. A more balanced approach to the self now begins to emerge as internal dialogue becomes less caustic. A posture of greater courage and comfort within the self is assumed by the adolescent as hang-ups and inhibitions about how they are perceived by others diminish.

Sixteen-year-old Gamila has secured a part-time job in a local pharmacy, working weekend shifts and occasional evenings after school. The tunic supplied to her is a size too big. She is mortified at how unshapely it makes her look but feels it would be rude to ask for a better-fitting uniform. Gamila doesn't want to cause any bother or be a burden. For the first few days, she worries obsessively about administering the incorrect medication to a customer and inadvertently killing them – before she realises that dispensing prescriptions is not part of her role. She is nervous about using the till in case she makes a mistake, overcharging people or losing money for the business. Other staff members and customers make conversation with the adolescent about the weather, readiness for Christmas and general small talk about life in their town. Gamila mostly feels awkward during these exchanges, struggling to think of what to say. Each year, during school holidays and then college summer breaks, she returns to work in the pharmacy. Over this time the adolescent evolves considerably in relation to the degree of comfort she experiences. Some mornings she doesn't have time to straighten her hair or put on make-up and it doesn't bother her in the slightest, in fact, during her shifts Gamila usually forgets about what she looks like as she is focused on doing her job. If she isn't sure about something, rather than worrying about screwing up, she readily asks for support. Gamila shows great initiative and engages in friendly banter with staff and customers alike. The adolescent now demonstrates a decidedly freer and more flexible approach to herself and to how she shows up in the world. The intensity and self-monitoring which characterised the inhibitive stage of her development is replaced by self-assurance and an ease in her relatedness.

Empathy and Relating

The adolescent's ability to empathise involves the frontal lobe region of the brain and this becomes more activated for young people whose configuration style is directional. Empathy is the ability to contain one's emotions and step out of the inclination to self-reference in order to conceive of someone else's subjective experience. The impulsive young person experiences emotions without much concern for other people's feelings, opening them up to situations such as heated exchanges with parents and bullying behaviour with peers. Conversely, the inhibitive adolescent tends to become overly sensitive to and negatively preoccupied with the feeling worlds of others, commonly with a narcissistic edge to their inferences. However, as directional adolescents become more surefooted, they are capable of more complex emotional processes and an increasing degree of relational maturity.

Adolescents now possess the potential to regulate their behaviour so that it is socially considered and appropriate, whilst also remaining true to themselves. As a younger impulsive adolescent Aidan readily participated in peer harassment of a few classmates, which was always guaranteed to generate a laugh. The only real consideration which mattered in relation to the impact of tormenting other boys was trying to be as funny as possible when doing so in order to maintain his status and belonging within his friendship group. Following the cool swagger of his impulsive years, a more self-conscious period was ushered in during the inhibitive stage of his developmental journey. Aidan's friends still mattered, but their significance in his life wasn't quite as figural now. The adolescent had developed a major crush on a girl who wasn't that interested. This gave rise to gnawing insecurity and a preoccupation with self-conscious comparison. He started out on a path of self-improvement in order to impress his love interest and spent endless hours wondering what she thought of him. Now, as Aidan reaches the shores of directional functioning, he is able to reassess his earlier engagement with peers. He is mortified at how he treated some boys in his class during his junior years and yearns to apologise and explain that he is, in fact, a decent human being. However, if he happens to bump into any of these young men, he finds that he avoids eye contact, such is his level of shame. Looking back at his infatuation with the girl during his inhibitive years, he smiles to himself as it dawns on him what a truly dreadful pairing they would have made. He is stunned at how much of his headspace and identity had been consumed by the pursuit of this relationship. The parent's plea to their younger teenager: *'What were you thinking?'* has now been replaced with the directional adolescent's wondering: *What the hell was I thinking??*

Personal Agency

Emergence of greater self-possession and equanimity means less self-doubt and uncertainty when navigating the world of social interaction. The directional adolescent remains innately resilient and their sense of identity is much less influenced by their peer environment. With more balanced insight into their lives and greater conscious awareness of themselves and others in their world, directional adolescents approach friendship and wider interpersonal contact on more solid psychological ground. The drama of earlier adolescence typically wanes and is replaced by mutuality, reciprocity and empathic consideration.

Personal and social responsibility come more clearly into focus as adolescents select courses of action and experiment with how to live personally meaningful lives. They become increasingly mindful of the future – *their future.* They begin figuring out in more concrete terms who they want to be, what they want to do, where and with whom they want their short- or longer-term lives to unfold. Freedom and independence present both choice and demand as they organise themselves with increasing courage, discipline and flexibility. The art is to remain present to their growing sense of personal integrity, creating consciously aware and purposeful lives. Directional adolescents are essentially moving in the right direction and, due to increased brain connectivity, have infinitely more stable lives than their impulsive or inhibitive counterparts.

Directional adolescents have a relative degree of faith in themselves and an optimism about their world. Their brains are steadily maturing and interconnecting, and with the frontal lobe in the driver's seat they are more inclined to approach life with potentially greater balance and perspective.

Let's take homework for example: Charlie is an impulsive adolescent and has zero inclination to study at home. He avoids starting and instead spends most of the evening gaming, which feels good. As he demonstrates no responsibility in relation to his homework, his concerned parents step in and the predictable battles ensue. His mum and dad are insufferable. Charlie doesn't care about the future. Life is about having fun, and the exams are an unnecessary distraction. He's going to become an influencer – you don't need academic qualifications for that. Charlie eventually does his homework because he's made to do it.

Michelle, an inhibitive adolescent, spends hours each night, and even more on the weekends, meticulously attending to homework. She is never sure if she's done enough so tends to overstudy and overprepare. If only her work ethic was complimented by some degree of faith in herself, Michelle's progress would feel more meaningful for her. She hates the pressure of academic life and feels suffocated by the sheer volume of work she has to complete. However, the adolescent does her homework because not to do it would be unthinkable and she is driven to do well – her self-esteem depends on her academic success. As top of her class, she remains competitive and feels stressed all the time trying to manage expectations.

Lauren, on the other hand, approaches her homework with a healthy and realistic attitude. She is directional and finds balance between having the discipline to apply herself to the task without overdoing it. Lauren figures that her homework will take a couple of hours. She can put the phone away and remain focused, whilst still having time to chill out afterwards. Once the homework is completed, she sets it aside for the remainder of her evening. The adolescent recognises its importance and at the same time can put it in perspective – there is also more to life than homework. Whilst Charlie is all about the feel-good, Lauren knows when to dial it down. And whereas Michelle has to be the best, Lauren gives it her best shot. There is a qualitative difference to each their approaches: the impulsive adolescent's approach to homework is undermotivated, so concerned adults step in and stressful power struggles ensue. The stakes are too high for the inhibitive adolescent whose escalating pressure levels are fuelled by inadequacy-driven perfectionism. The directional adolescent takes her studies seriously and is both disciplined and measured in her approach. Her sense of self is not tied to either her efforts or her performance.

The Consistently Directional Adolescent

Plenty of young people who demonstrate a directional configuration style have episodes of impulsivity or inhibition. We refer to them as sensible, considerate and mature – and they are, for the most part. They possess an inherent sense of security and tend to be natural leaders. They fit comfortably and fluently within the peer landscape, take themselves seriously – but not too seriously – and manage to maintain relatively close supportive contact with the adult world. They display a positive and even-tempered attitude towards their lives and tend not to be thrown too much off-balance when there are developmental wobbles.

Caitlin has always been a composed and level-headed adolescent who has a good group of friends and gets on well with her parents and teachers. She engages in academic life without much drama and is mostly agreeable at home. When issues surface, she consults with adults and learns to become a good problem solver. Whilst she enjoys her social life, she usually knows where to draw the line. Caitlin enjoys nights out with her friends and occasionally overindulges. On the evening of her senior year ball, she got so drunk that she spent most of the night passed out. And whilst her parents were less than impressed, indulging of impulses is not an ongoing issue. Caitlin also experiences anxiety at times, though it is proportionate to the circumstances in which she finds herself. For example, when her father goes through a period of ill health or before important exams, the adolescent feels off-balance and nearing overwhelm. When these situations pass, her anxiety recedes and she is back to her positive, relatively stable and directional self again. The adolescent would like to be a little thinner and a little taller, and whilst this bothers her to some extent, Caitlin does not let it define her self-experience. She is mostly able to see beyond her physical frame, her academic success and her other achievements and experience herself as so much more than simply these external attributes. When the adolescent has 'ugly days' or sometimes doesn't do as well as she had hoped, she is rattled. However, she doesn't collapse. Due to bigger-picture thinking, a kinder relationship to herself and the capacity to regulate emotional arousal, directional adolescents demonstrate innate resilience.

Directionality as a Creative Adjustment

Sometimes young people grow up in homes where other family members' needs take precedence, for whatever reason. These adolescents may demonstrate a directional configuration style as other family members are afforded a disproportionate amount of time and attention. The adolescent develops self-reliance, becoming trustworthy and responsible beyond their years. Their directional nature and level of maturity have to do with suppression of their own needs. These adolescents don't give anyone any bother because they implicitly understand that they have to be OK – there is no room to be otherwise. Family life unfolds in ways which tend to leave them overlooked.

Fourteen-year-old Dylan's younger sister received a diagnosis of autism aged five. By nine years of age, Mia's presentation also suggested Bipolar Disorder, however her psychiatrist was reluctant to diagnose at such a young age. Mia struggles with crippling anxiety and is very dependent on her mother for reassurance and psychological support. The child feels terrorised when she perceives even a hint of threat to her comfort zone. Mia struggles with school, friendships and sleep. She lives in dreaded fear of something happening to her mother, of making mistakes, of burglars and of dying. The child feels somewhat soothed when in close proximity to her mother and finds it difficult to share her mum with her brother and dad. Emotional dysregulation means that Mia's moods are unpredictable, with prolonged temper tantrums and meltdowns an almost daily feature of family life.

Helping Mia feel better doesn't come as naturally to her father. As a consequence, he is expelled from the child's comfort zone and essentially alienated by his daughter. Dad is an easy-going person and sings to himself around the house – usually the wrong words of songs and often out of tune. This dements Mia who also can't tolerate the sound of him breathing or chewing. And so, much of her explosive rages are directed at him. Mia's parents are very concerned about her mental health and aggressive behaviour. This is the focus of much of their dialogue, which usually ends in them arguing about their divergent and equally ineffective parenting strategies. There are endless appointments with mental health professionals, educators and complementary therapists in the search for some intervention that might make a difference.

In the meantime, Dylan has himself together and is very even-keeled. He tends not to make demands on his parents, for he understands that they are already overwhelmed with attending to Mia's needs. He has become artful at recognising the first signs of an approaching tornado and has learned to remove himself when Mia is on the cusp of another blowout. Dylan's contact with his younger sister amounts to placating her and avoiding contention, as she is impatient and unable to compromise. The adolescent is an industrious student and spends a good deal of time in his room, either studying or on screens. He tends not to invite friends round as Mia inevitably spoils the experience by creating a scene. Dylan's parents love him dearly and are very grateful that he is a much easier child to rear. His mother often repeats the phrase, *'Thank god Dylan gives us no bother.'* Her statement reminds Dylan that being a good and loveable son means not asking for his needs to be met and reinforces his posture of having to be 'fine'.

Out of the blue one day, Dylan asks if he can talk to a therapist. His parents are taken aback as he doesn't seem to have any issues – he is happy, doing well in school, enjoys sport and has a good bunch of friends. Nothing ever seems to bother him. When I meet Dylan, I am impressed with the fourteen-year-old's level of maturity and capacity for dialogue. He assures me that he is fine and says that he isn't really sure why he wanted to come. I invite the adolescent to share his experience of his life and his response is: *'I don't have a life. My life is all about Mia.'*

Dylan bursts into tears and sobs for much of the session. He is exhausted living with Mia's hyperarousal, and it pains him to see how bankrupted of energy and joy his parents have become. He understands why he is overlooked and wears it gracefully, however, underneath his positive demeanour Dylan is broken-hearted at having insufficient attention, emotional support and time with his parents. The adolescent creatively adjusts to his family situation by denying his needs. Inside, he feels lost and unseen.

The experience of trauma can also catapult adolescents into a directional configuration style prematurely. Distressing experiences can trigger an impulsive or inhibitive reaction, however some adolescents creatively adjust to the presence of trauma by stepping up to the plate. Sixteen-year-old Colm's older brother was murdered on a night out with friends which devastates his family. Prior to this situation, Colm very definitely demonstrated an impulsive configuration style: he regularly got drunk, took drugs and scraped by in school. His social life and having fun were everything to him. When his brother, whom he looked up to, dies, Colm makes the decision to start taking himself seriously and to live his life in a manner which will make his deceased sibling proud. The adolescent knuckles down in school, reins in his social life and changes the focus of his life. He demonstrates impressive maturity, a tremendous loyalty to his family and a generous community spirit. When I meet him, Colm is completing a PhD in engineering, the path of study his older brother had chosen.

Similarly, adolescents who live directionally may creatively adjust by becoming entrenched in another configuration style in response to difficult circumstances. Cara is one such young person who is a bright, compassionate and mature adolescent when she starts dating David. As an entrenched inhibitive adolescent, David is obsessive, highly self-referenced and very insecure. His intensifying jealousy and subtle criticism of Cara create a lot of stress and uncertainty for her. This results in her feeling bad about herself, cutting off contact with friends and trying to please her boyfriend more and more. Cara loses faith in herself, feels inadequate and her self-confidence evaporates. She has developed an inhibitive configuration style and resembles a shell of her former self. Therapy supports her to explore the dynamics and impact of her relationship with David. In time, she finds the courage to walk away and heal from the effects of David's narcissistic influence, becoming directional once more.

Flexibility versus Entrenchment

The directional configuration style is defined by greater emotional balance, psychological stability and relational maturity. However, nobody remains directional at all times, undeviating from integrated frontal lobe activation. That would be the definition of a perfect human being and, as far as we know, none exist. Impulsive expression and inhibitive preoccupation can dominate from time to time and this is to be expected of even the most sensible, stable directional adolescent. As adulthood begins to come into view over the horizon, adolescents' lives are principally directed from the frontal lobe (hopefully) though they continue to get ambushed by urges and strong feelings. That's why they break diets, can't be bothered to work on a college dissertation or fall away from the gym. They have a hankering for something sweet, a visit to the library will wait until tomorrow and they'll get back to their exercise regime next month. During these times the limbic system is dominating self-process. Conversely, directional adolescents are prone to getting themselves into inhibitive binds every now and again. They stay awake at night worrying about their travel plans to Australia, feel terribly insecure in relation to a love interest or panic when going for job interviews. Though mostly they demonstrate an ever-increasing degree of psychological balance.

This flexible movement and shifting between the various configuration styles is a natural process, giving colour and identity to our lives. However, this integrated and fluid way of being should not be confused with entrenched modes of functioning. For example, Brian has received a diagnosis of ADD and struggles with impulse control and emotional regulation. He goes head-to-head with parents on most issues and seems to be perpetually in trouble. Brian's limbic system is a force to be reckoned with and powerfully influences his experience of himself and the world. As well as ADD, Brian has a co-existing anxiety disorder and there are also times where he displays excessive anxiety and dread. He shifts from one entrenched mode of being to another, recycling through episodes of impulsivity and inhibition.

Aisling, on the other hand, is a staunchly inhibitive adolescent and worries her way through life. Exhibiting the usual characteristics of perfectionism in the face of inadequacy and a propensity to overthink, she endures ongoing anxiety symptoms and her sense of self is dominated by a still-maturing cerebral cortex which creates intensity and self-conscious rumination. When she senses she is at the edge of her comfort zone, the brain's alert system – the amygdala, situated in the limbic system – whips her up into a state of hyperarousal. The normally timorous Aisling cries, screams, shouts, kicks out and generally loses control in response to emotional distress. When overwhelmed, the adolescent's brain changes mode and becomes limbic-activated, evidenced by frequent meltdowns. Aisling's entrenched inhibitive configuration style makes her prone to becoming limbic-activated, though like Brian, there is little sign of developmental progression. Rather than demonstrating psychological flexibility with flashes of impulsive and inhibitive processes, Brian's and Aisling's shifting between limbic and cerebral cortex regions of the brain is evidence of entrenched functioning. Both adolescents demonstrate rigidity and demand life on their terms, though are guided by very different motivations: the impulsive adolescent wants to feel good and belong and isn't interested in participating in anything that doesn't stimulate his dopamine flow; the inhibitive adolescent organises her lifespace to feel as much comfort and as little threat as possible in order to keep pressure and anxiety to a minimum. Flexibility, on the other hand, is a hallmark of a healthy, relatively balanced individual and suggests a directional configuration style. Hopefully, over time both adolescents will continue to evolve in a more directional manner, though this is not a given. For some who endure entrenchment, reaching adulthood does not equate with being directional. The capacity for optimal brain connectivity and achievement of a directional configuration style remains elusive and whilst they look like adults, they remain governed by limbic or immature cerebral cortex energy. Not all grown-ups are adults.

If I Knew Then What I Know Now

Being impulsive can be great fun but it usually also spells some kind of trouble. Some of the calls adolescents make are questionable to say the least and can reverberate, causing shame-shivers right into adulthood: antics on drunken nights out, regretted sexual encounters, bullying behaviour, being horrible to parents, not taking school seriously. Similarly, cerebral cortex activity locks adolescents in a mental prison and they tend to become their own worst enemy. Looking back on the inhibitive stage of being a teenager, people lament the fact that they were so unnecessarily self-conscious and so very hard on themselves. They wish they hadn't worried so much about everything.

Directional adolescents develop the capacity to respond to life with greater balance and perspective. They have self-confidence, resilience and a security in themselves and in their worlds. As they reach the shores of adulthood and reflect back on their adolescent journey, some people say: *'I'm so glad I'm not a teenage anymore. They were supposed to be the best years of your life, but for me they were miserable and messy.'* Others remark, *'I'd love to go back to my teenage years and do it all again…and this time I'd do it all so very differently.'* What the latter group actually mean to say is: *'I'd love to have gone through my adolescence wholly frontal lobe-activated and with fully adult consideration of my life and my choices.'*

There is potential for shame at every turn for adolescents as they make their way from childhood to adulthood and this unrealistic fantasy usually relates to a yearning to heal the shame endured and caused during those tender and vulnerable teenage years. For most, adolescence involves periods of impulsivity and inhibition, with gradual advancement towards a *mostly* directional configuration style. As well as fond memories, retrospective embarrassment and the shame-shivers are natural for most adults when we consider our adolescent journey, if we're honest.

Part 2

The Parent

The Parquet

Part 2

Chapter 6

Understanding Parents

Being a fully functional adult suggests that a person has reached a relatively solid, stable sense of self and level of organisation within their lifespace. Impulsivity which is modulated through self-discipline continues to ensure spontaneity, pleasure and the vibrancy of an emotional connection with self and the world. A capacity for reflection, empathic perception and purposeful living is supported through whole brain connectivity.

Quite often, being a directional adult also means having a wing of impulsivity or inhibition. For example, Lynn is a mature, responsible adult who is in charge of her life…except when it comes to food. She makes excellent decisions influenced by her frontal cortex in virtually all aspects of her life, but with regards to food she is governed by her limbic system. She follows diets, joins weight-loss groups, has a library of healthy eating books and is virtually as knowledgeable as a professional nutritionist. Nevertheless, she can't shift her impulsive relationship to food. Lynn has the best intentions, though when it comes to it, she doesn't *feel* like eating the healthy salad…instead she opens the fridge and asks herself, *What do I* feel *like eating? I* fancy *some chocolate. I'd* love *pizza tonight.* She battles this spontaneous relationship with food and no matter how hard Lynn tries to control her impulsivity, she inevitably falls off the wagon. Consequently, regret and disgust kick in as she relentlessly berates herself for being undisciplined and overweight. Lynn's sense of self is tied up with an oppressive hostility about her body shape and deep concern about her health. She knows that if she could master her diet, she would feel much better about herself and it would free up considerable headspace. Lynn is directional and relates as an adult within her lifespace, apart from this dimension of her life when limbic activity gets the upper hand.

I suspect that most healthy functioning adults have a wing of impulsivity or inhibition, or both. However, being principally directional is not a universal attribute of adult life. *It is a developmental achievement, not a developmental certainty.* As people become older, some may look like grown-ups, though their capacity to function as psychologically mature adults is questionable. Lots of people remain entrenched in impulsive or inhibitive configuration styles, experiencing only momentary episodes of directional functioning. The feelings, thoughts and memories which inform their sense of self also infuse their relationships. When

DOI: 10.4324/9781003373599-9

impulsive and inhibitive people become parents, their respective approaches can be somewhat predictable. It is useful to understand this parenting context as it will inform parental involvement work for the therapist.

The Impulsive Parent

Greg has a great day planned for Tyler, his fourteen-year-old teenage son. They start off with breakfast in town on Saturday morning before heading for the rugby match in Dublin later that afternoon. Father and son enjoy a great connection during their day out and feel close to each other. Greg is responsive, attuned and present as a dad. He is feeling great and is buzzing from the enjoyment they are having together. He asks his son if he would like to go bowling next Saturday – which is something he feels like he really wants to do. Tyler is looking forward to it too. By the end of the week, however, Greg has forgotten his commitment. He goes out for a few drinks on Friday evening and is nursing a hangover on Saturday. He doesn't feel like going bowling, so he tells his son he'll take him another time. It's months before this comes to pass.

Greg, an impulsive parent, is the best dad in the world…when he *feels* like it. Parenting is on his terms and is characterised by emotionality and inconsistency. When he comes in from work his son wonders to himself, *What kind of mood is dad in this evening?* If he is in an emotionally balanced or cheerful space, or when he's buzzing, he is a wonderful dad, and everyone will have a great evening. If he is off-balance with stress or darker emotions such as sadness, frustration or anger, dad's feeling world will dictate family life for the evening. Greg is governed by limbic activity, with his moods determining each interaction with his teenage son. Dad is so wrapped up in his need for dopamine and in his own narrative that Tyler has grown used to tolerating a relationship on his father's terms. It sometimes feels like an all-or-nothing scenario for the adolescent who has learned to ride the highs and lows of being parented by Greg. Today could be enriching and nurturing for Tyler…if dad is in a good mood and feels like engaging as a parent. It is equally likely that he will experience the familiar feelings of disappointment and contempt for his dad from being overlooked or devoured by Greg again. As Greg's parenting is largely dictated by his feelings, this creates a chaotic energy in his relationship with his son. He can become off-balance in an instant which leads to unpredictable moods and emotional reactivity. Tyler has learned to figure out his dad's mood so that he knows where he stands with him at any moment. The adolescent is learning not to expect his needs to be met and that love, and relationships, are conditional. He is also developing the art of relational hypervigilence.

Adults who experience ongoing entrenched impulsivity demonstrate emotional immaturity. All is well when Tyler is easy to parent. However, the adolescent, at fourteen, is himself impulsively configured and disposed to doing only what he feels like doing. His level of compliance to parental requests is questionable and he is prone to risk-taking and getting into trouble. Parents need to have a lot of patience when their teenagers are impulsive. However, Greg's self-experience is organised through this configuration style too. When he is provoked by Tyler's behaviour, dad is set quickly off-balance and becomes emotionally reactive. He shouts, demands, has rage attacks, huffs and ignores his son. The pair experience frequent 'limbic parties' where both are immersed in their feeling worlds without space to reflect and be choiceful. In these moments, both of them behave like teenagers – appropriate for Tyler, not for dad – and there are times when it almost comes to blows between them.

A limbic-activated parent's contact with their teenage child is often unintentionally antagonistic. Geraldine's daughter Shauna struggles with impulse control much of the time. This shows up in friendships, academic work and relationships with family members. If Shauna doesn't get her own way, this usually ends in a meltdown. She has gotten into trouble with bullying, unsafe activity on her phone, disruptive class behaviour and experimentation with alcohol. Her mother Geraldine relies on the strategies of nagging, lecturing, threatening and punishment to manage Shauna's impulsive behaviour. When the adolescent is sitting in her bedroom on her phone, Geraldine comes in:

'Look at the shape of this room, get that tidied and bring those dishes down to the kitchen. I don't know how you live in this room; it's disgusting. I want you to do the floors – run the hoover over the downstairs rooms and mop the kitchen floor. Put that phone away when I'm talking to you and don't roll your eyes at me young lady. Do you hear what I'm saying? Get up and do what I say. NOW.'

Fifteen minutes later, Shauna hasn't budged, because she is happy where she is and doesn't feel like doing housework. Geraldine re-enters the bedroom this time with more aggression and impatience in her tone:

'Get downstairs this instant and do as you're told. I told you to get the floors cleaned. I come in from work and I have the whole house to do and the dinner to make. The least you could do is give me a bit of a hand when I ask you. You're good for nothing sitting about all day on that phone. I'll not ask you again. GET DOWNSTAIRS NOW!'

A screaming match ensues as a highly defensive mother and daughter hurl insults and accusations at one another. Past experiences are dredged up, adding fuel to the fire, and each gives as good as they get in this ugly exchange. Afterwards, Geraldine approaches her husband for support. Finbar is a quiet, passive man who tries to remain uninvolved and is inevitably recruited as peacekeeper between the pair. Geraldine expresses her upset about her lazy, disrespectful, selfish daughter. She asks Finbar to speak to her daughter and when he says *'She's just young; she'll grow out of it'* Geraldine rails at her husband's failure to take her side, berating him for being useless and leaving the parenting all to her.

Later that evening, Shauna is in the living room watching TV. Geraldine enters the room, takes the remote control and turns the television off. Shauna is immediately activated and off-balance because she was enjoying a programme. Geraldine looks sternly at her daughter: *'Well, have you anything to say for yourself?'*

Her mother proceeds to give Shauna a lecture about the importance of obeying her parents and pulling her weight around the house. Geraldine tells the adolescent that she feels like she is being treated as a slave in her own home and that this will have to stop. She asks for an apology. And another thing, Shauna is going to have to start knuckling down to her studies and spending less time on her screens. The adolescent has heard this bunch of bullshit for the hundredth time. She puts her hood up and rolls her eyes. This signals round two of the evening's battle, after which Geraldine announces that she is washing her hands of her daughter and is having nothing more to do with her. It is three weeks before she speaks directly to Shauna again.

This mother's entrenched impulsivity creates a lack of measured insight into her daughter's behaviour and lack of capacity to form a reasoned response when things don't go well. Her contact is antagonistic and triggers oppositional and reactive behaviour from Shauna who endures a lot of blaming and shaming. Mum is convinced that Shauna's attitude is the issue, however Geraldine's parenting approach is contentious and destructive. The situation is certainly not all of Shauna's making and to work individually with the adolescent, failing to address parental antagonism, risks colluding with this mother. Therapeutic intervention will aim to support both mother and daughter to become more considered and less reactive in their relating.

Impulsive parents have a reputation for being challenging, as the therapist often has to manage some level of chaos. Less experienced therapists, in particular, can struggle with these dynamics. Engagement in therapy can be impacted by the parent's characteristic lack of consistency, as appointments are missed, or younger children are brought along to meetings. The parent can initially be very grateful that a professional is going to intervene and solve their problems, even putting the therapist on a pedestal. It is usually not long before mum or dad, who becomes dysregulated when parenting does not go to plan, begins to lean on the therapist for support. A dependent energy may emerge where the parent is emailing the therapist out of hours to let her know what went wrong or calling her at 8.45am frantic that her teenager won't get out of the car and go into school. In desperation she asks the therapist, *'What should I do?'* Urgency infuses the therapeutic space and drives the therapist to over-reach.

Therapists may decide to meet a parent briefly at the beginning of a session and ask how things have been, only to find that twenty-five minutes later the mother is still talking about herself. The therapist struggles to contain the mother's narrative, as well as her own judgement and frustration as she reacts to how the parent appears oblivious to the fact that this is the adolescent's time and space. The reactive energy which characterises parenting experience starts to infuse the therapist's posture and gives rise to bias, power struggling and frustration. Parental inconsistency and ongoing emotional reactivity are the major obstacles when engaging impulsive parents in an adolescent psychotherapy process. Transitioning to a new parenting stance is effortful and requires commitment, qualities which are notoriously difficult for the impulsive parent to consistently demonstrate. Therapists commonly have a sense that the parent needs therapy more than the adolescent and knows that the strategies she is offering would work if only the parent possessed the insight, emotional containment and consistency to see them through.

The Inhibitive Parent

Adults who continue to demonstrate an inhibitive configuration style tend to experience disconnection from their emotional world and have a pragmatic approach to life and to parenting. There is often a narcissistic edge to their relating. Colette's externalised sense of self extends to her relationship with her teenage daughter Bethany. Mum says that she just wants Bethany to be happy, though seems preoccupied with the adolescent's grades and achievements – encouraging the adolescent's performance and outward success. When Bethany struggles with self-doubt, her mother responds by giving her solutions and misses cues for emotional mirroring and validation.

Bethany: 'Mum I'm feeling really worried about going to school tomorrow. I've a sore stomach and I'm just so anxious.'
Mum: 'Don't worry about it. Once you get there, you'll be fine.'
Bethany: 'But what if I fail the test? I so worried about letting everyone down.'
Mum: 'Tell you what, I'll quiz you on what you have revised and see how you get on. If you need to revise more, then you have a couple of hours this evening to go back over anything you weren't sure of.'
Bethany: 'But the girls aren't speaking to me, I'll feel awkward when I'm in class with them tomorrow.'
Mum: 'Those girls are just rude. You're better off without them, just put your head in the air and walk on.'

Colette, though well-intentioned, lacks self-awareness and emotional depth and so, struggles to recognise and support her daughter's emotional development. Parenting for Colette is about solving problems and emphasising academic and material success. Outward progress equates to good parenting and, as a result, her teenager's emotional world tends to be neglected. She is very busy in the world, with a tendency to overschedule her family's life and has zero capacity to relax. When the family sit down to dinner each evening, dialogue is focused on activities and scheduling: what people are *doing* rather than how they are *experiencing* themselves and their world. Colette is an immensely attentive and committed parent – perhaps a little too entangled in her children's lives at times. Mum's focus on creating a perceived family culture which is acceptable outside the home and her tendency to be emotionally withholding results in Bethany not feeling known to her mother. This lack of validation leaves the adolescent preoccupied with making sure that her external world is acceptable and ever conscious about what others think of her. And so, the family pattern of inhibitive functioning continues.

When Colette reaches out to me for support for her daughter's anxiety, her expectation is that the process will involve the application of a bunch of anxiety-reducing techniques and that I will offer a quick fix – after all that's my job. Mum is very focused on symptoms and solutions and shows up to sessions eager to be enlightened by my expertise. Colette asks plenty of questions about the symptoms, wonders whether I have seen this type of presentation before and enquires as to how long the course of treatment will take. This mother approaches her daughter's anxiety symptoms as a problem to be solved and I get a sense of Colette's two-dimensional understanding of her daughter's presentation.

Meeting with Colette and her daughter, I attempt to deepen the dialogue, picking up this inhibitive parent's slight discomfort as the conversation moves into more obscure and potentially vulnerable territory. Focusing on relational patterns, I invite Colette to reflect on what kind of a teenager she was herself and to describe the relationship between mother and daughter. Colette tolerates this part of the conversation out of politeness, though feels mildly frustrated at the irrelevance of this line of questioning. She thinks I am missing the point; but for the me, this *is* the point. There is a notable lack of depth to the mother's responses and when Colette is asked how she *feels*, she responds by describing what she *thinks*. I intuit a general lack of comfort and openness in Colette's presentation and sense of self. Contact with this inhibitive parent feels limited as she struggles to step into a more reflective mode and relinquish her urgency to fix.

Understandably, a parent's quasi-involvement in the process is likely to provoke reaction in the therapist who is starting out. Sitting with an inhibitive parent can feel pressuring and deskilling, as the therapist wrestles with feelings of inadequacy and an urgency to deliver the goods. The adolescent therapist can feel rather bombarded and may judge the parent as overbearing. The pressure which saturates Colette and Bethany's world has begun to infuse the therapeutic space. The practitioner is all about feelings, empathy and experience, so it is jolting to encounter someone who thinks, rather than feels, their way through life. The therapist might well conclude that the parent is on the autistic spectrum and that it would be easier to not involve the parent in any ongoing work, though that is likely not the most effective way forward.

The Directional Parent

Parents whose self-experience is filtered through the frontal cortex are grounded, balanced and emotionally receptive. They intuitively understand how they need to show up in their child's life in order to create security, mirroring and resilience. To be sure, adolescence can bring with it plenty of potential for a directional parent to become non-receptive, though this tends to happen without the ugly showdowns and the powerlessness which characterise the parenting experience with the more impulsive and inhibitive adolescents.

John's daughter Elaine has become a handful during early adolescence. He is concerned about her attitude. The teenager has become disagreeable, has started hanging around with impulsive peers and is experimenting with vaping and alcohol. Her grades have dropped, and the school have also noted a deterioration in her general attitude. He understands that something is up with his daughter, though he's not sure exactly what. Dad's contact with Elaine is non-shaming for the most part. He remains emotionally responsive and not reactive in volatile situations, though he's tearing his hair out in private about this shift in his daughter's demeanour. There is some nagging and lecturing, though John senses that Elaine may benefit from speaking to someone.

When John and Elaine arrive at the initial appointment, there is an openness and awareness to the father's contact. He explains to me that both he and his daughter need some support – there is no scapegoating of the adolescent. Without shame, he takes ownership of the fact that his parenting is less than influential just now and engages as a willing participant in the dialogue. He gets that there is a context, developmental or otherwise, to his daughter's attitude shift. Rather than listing her misdemeanours and concerning behaviours, this dad is interested in finding a way to make his daughter's path, and their contact, less fraught. John readily reflects on his relationship with his daughter and on his parenting approach. This father will do whatever it takes to support his daughter and will continue to show up with considered and collaborative participation, open to taking on board and implementing any parenting advice and strategies he receives. The inexperienced therapist finds that this directional parent's non-defensive posture and self-awareness make him an easy person to like. She may have a more casual style of relating with him than with the other parents she encounters and wishes that all parents she meets could be like John.

Parent as Traumatiser

When a parent's entrenched impulsive or inhibitive configuration style is extreme, they create unsafety and distress within the adolescent's lifespace. During their earliest days of existence, the adolescent is likely to have learned to dissociate in the spirit of self-preservation, in response to a parent being the source of overwhelm. Parentally traumatised adolescents are amygdala-driven and tend to compromise their sense of self. The adolescent journey becomes less about development and more about survival as the person nominated to nurture and create safety generates the opposite experience, devastating the young person. The parental relationship is an unsafe, threatening and abusive relational space.

Ideally the therapist will involve parents whenever she can for the purpose of creating increased empathy for and attunement to their adolescent children, supporting parents to understand and let go of approaches which do not serve the best interests of either their teenager's developmental location or the parent-adolescent relationship. This attempt to foster greater awareness and receptivity requires a level of willingness to reflect on one's parenting style and to potentially make some changes in a spirit of support for the teenager. One, however, must be realistic. The sad reality is that there are situations in which it is not a sound call to engage parents in any meaningful manner. Concerns related to safety and reliability are figural here and it is the case that some parents are so disturbed in themselves that their involvement is contraindicated.

Generational Trauma

The dualistic notion of good and bad parents is unhelpful and overly simplistic. Some children grow up in dysfunctional families, enduring the unacknowledged and projected pain of generational trauma. This specific term relates to the legacy and direct impact of historical traumatic experiences which affect younger generations within families. Many people who suffered dreadfully as children find the resources and support to live happy, meaningful lives. Sadly, some continue to live under the imprint of generational trauma, creating disruptive, unsafe relationships with their own children. As adults they are haunted by the burden of traumatic memories which shapes their sense of self. Their capacity, as human beings, to transcend this suffering and not live their lives defined by it, is miraculous. However, some people require intensive support to work through these generational wounds, undergoing radical healing and transformation before the adolescent therapist may consider it appropriate to extend an invitation for them to engage in the therapeutic process. Realistically this level of support is rarely an option.

The adolescent is at the heart of the therapeutic space at all times and recruiting traumatising parents may compromise or threaten the adolescent's experience of being held by the therapist. If the adolescent's safety and wellbeing are at stake, then it may be unhelpful to include some parents in the therapeutic work.

The Impulsive Traumatising Parent

Peter grew up in a violent, alcoholic home and spent his adolescence entrenched in limbic energy, not taking either himself or life particularly seriously. In his early twenties he emigrated from Ireland to the United States, working on building sites and in his uncle's bar. He learned to work hard and party hard. He met his wife there and they returned to Ireland after eight years. The couple's social life was great at the start of their relationship and they were very much in love. Before long they were expecting their first child Luke, who now at sixteen years of age has found his way to my office. As soon as she discovered the pregnancy, Maureen made changes to her lifestyle. She stopped drinking and her emphasis shifted from socialising to homemaking. Peter didn't seem to register that parenthood was approaching and continued with his partying lifestyle. As the father's drinking became more problematic Maureen complained, which resulted in Peter becoming increasingly frustrated. This evolved into violence within their relationship and the full force of generational trauma was felt within Peter's family. Luke and his siblings witnessed their father direct abuse in all its forms towards their mother. Peter's primary connection was with alcohol and this shaped family contact. He was a grumpy, disinterested and abrasive parent whose explosive rages created terror for his family. As a child, Luke was both hurt and relieved that his father did not demonstrate more care and interest in his son.

Frontal cortex integration makes for good parenting and Peter's entrenched limbic activity means that he lacks empathy, attunement and a sense of parental responsibility. His parenting is characterised by emotional volatility, immature behaviour, addiction and dislocation. He possesses few of the developmental requirements for attuned parenting.

As a younger child, Luke yearned for his dad to stop drinking and creating so much carnage. However, a parent's toxic impulsivity frequently gives way to detachment during adolescence. Now, he doesn't care. The adolescent has learned to subdue his yearning for his dad to show up the way he needs him to and has replaced this yearning with indifference. It is of no consequence to him whether his dad gets sober or kills himself drinking. In fact, as contempt sets in, fantasies about his father dying are common for the adolescent. Luke's childhood memories include gathering his siblings and running next door to his grandmother's house when his dad became violent with his mother; being taken to bars and having to sit there for hours whilst his dad got drunk; or being beaten and shamed for minor misdemeanours.

The adolescent has been referred following a recent diagnosis of depression and I express my preference to meet both parents along with the adolescent during the initial assessment. Peter attends though remains relatively detached throughout. I sense dad's tacit irritation with being involved and whilst Peter appears to say all the right things, I note a lack of empathy in his dialogue and a remoteness in his demeanour. A defensive wall protects this father during the meeting and my sense is that he is more enduring than participating in the dialogue. As is often the case when sitting with traumatising parents, the dialogue feels tight and closed down. Clarity about what family life is actually like for everyone remains elusive. Therapists often feel somewhat intimidated and unsettled during these encounters, breathing easier and feeling much less tense once the parent has exited the room.

The Inhibitive Traumatising Parent

Ken grew up in a repressive, religious household with an authoritarian father and loving but submissive mother. His parents modelled a strong work ethic, so as well as helping out on the family farm, Ken was expected to study hard. As a child, the adults in his world did not respond to his vulnerability or need to be emotionally validated, and so he developed an extremely rigid way of being in the world. Ken identified with his intellectual prowess but was emotionally shut down. His lack of being mirrored by parents created in him a very brittle sense of self and a lack of capacity to recognise anyone else's feeling world. As a result, in adulthood he demonstrates an arrogant, unempathic relationship to others and has a strong narcissistic tendency.

Ken owns a legal practice and works very hard. Whilst he has plenty of acquaintances through his work and church membership, he does not have any close friends. Anyone with less professional and social status is deemed inferior, and he is cynical and resentful of those who appear more successful than him. Ken met his wife Dorothy at university, and they have two adolescent children. Preoccupied with his family's outward success, Ken became chairperson of the Board of Governors of both the local primary and secondary schools which his son and daughter attended. His social standing as a successful solicitor, upstanding member of the church and active involvement within the school community means that Ken is a respected member of society. His valuable contribution to humanity does not, however, extend to his wife and children.

Ken and Dorothy built a house next door to his parents' home on the farm and the family lived there until the couple separated after fourteen years of marriage. Family life became increasingly problematic due to Ken's withholding of love, attention and acceptance of his children. This father's emotional immaturity is such that he parents without empathy. At home, Ken's modus operandi was violence and coercive control. When a family member set a foot wrong, according to his unreasonable notions, he reacted in an unsafe and shaming manner. Ken continues to relate to his children as extensions of himself, projecting his perfectionism and high expectations on to them. His mode of contact has encouraged the cultivation of an externalised sense of self for his son and daughter – the pain of growing up with insufficient validation and acceptance has translated into feelings of being unlovable, unworthy, defective, unacceptable and inadequate.

Andrew, the couple's second child, is referred for therapy during adolescence as his lack of confidence and paralysing social anxiety are becoming increasingly problematic. He is an extremely bright teenager, though is deeply uncomfortable in himself and finds relating to others an overwhelming experience. Once he finds his voice, the adolescent recounts many incidents of his father's deliberately destructive treatment of his son. As a four-year-old child, Andrew soiled himself after his father raged at him for accidentally breaking a plate at breakfast. Ken beat his son viciously, locked him in the bathroom and ordered him to clean himself up. Andrew was not allowed out of the bathroom until the next evening when dad came home from work. He cried himself to sleep, hungry, half-naked and frozen in the bath. He recalled his father driving him home from school, screaming and shouting at him for the entire journey because Andrew got a B plus in a maths class test. His father was furious, and the adolescent felt pinned to the seat, unable to escape his father's wrath. At the dinner table each evening, conversation felt more like cross-examination by his father and the tension was palpable as the adolescent waited to be attacked. Andrew regularly felt frightened and annihilated in the presence of his father.

Following parental separation Andrew resided with his mother, choosing to rarely see his father. However, the feeling of being unsafe continues to infuse his contact with others. He is utterly terrified in the world. Andrew's social anxiety is a symptom of having been parentally traumatised. The adolescent is feeling the full force of generational trauma and blames himself for his struggles. I experience the father's interactions as interrogating and provocative. Ken demonstrates no capacity for reflection and wants only reports of how the therapy is progressing. His lack of warmth and empathy, and the intimidating quality of his presence, affords me useful insight into Andrew's experience of being parented by this person.

Chapter 7

Parenting the Impulsive Adolescent

Rearing an impulsive teenager is not a particularly rewarding time in the life of a parent, although with all the moods and melodrama, it certainly is memorable. As childhood begins to dismantle, parents may experience the approaching teenage years as a loss in the relationship with their offspring. They miss the child who trusted them implicitly, opened up willingly and was such an affectionate and loving youngster. They yearn for that close connection once again as they witness how their little darling has, gradually or abruptly, been replaced by a sleep-bingeing, eye-rolling, smart-mouthed teenager who tells them nothing about their life and engages with them only when they want something. Parents, who had previously been cherished, tend to lose their status as role models and are unceremoniously toppled off their pedestals.

It is easy to feel loved by a younger child, less so by a teenager. For example, when dad arrives home from work his five-year-old son runs to the door to greet him with a hug and gushes about how he missed and is so very pleased to see him. The little chap spends the rest of the evening following his parent around the house. Dad's arrival home for the adolescent, however, is decidedly less enthusiastic. He might be lucky if his son lifts his head at all from the game console and has to be cajoled into even saying hello. Or the eight-year-old whose best friend is her mum, and whose intention it is to build a house right next door when she grows up, so that they will always be together. A handful of years later, the cuteness is gone, and she now adopts a scornful look when mum enters the sacred sanctuary of her teenage bedroom. She is mortified to be seen in public with this embarrassing and clueless woman. The adolescent cannot wait to escape her mother's clutches and leave this small-minded town when she is eighteen, never to return. Social distancing is not a new phenomenon created in the recent pandemic – adolescents have been practising it with their parents for generations!

How Parents Describe Their Impulsive Teens

It is not unusual for parents to experience loneliness and hurt during the teenage years, feeling frozen out when new boundaries start to emerge, and parents are no

DOI: 10.4324/9781003373599-10

longer cool. Whilst it is developmentally expected and reflects a young person who is right on track in relation to their lifespace journey, it is difficult at times not to take this rejection personally. A common complaint I hear in my office from parents is that their teenage children feel unreachable:

'He never talks to us; we don't know very much about his life. He won't even eat dinner with us and spends most of his time with his friends or locked in his bedroom. When we try to talk to him, he just rolls his eyes or tells us to leave him alone.'

When I start working with an adolescent, I meet with them and their parents together for the initial assessment. One of the first things I do is to invite the parents to broadly describe their teenager. Identifying that the young person is impulsive is a very straightforward process – parents will predictably use three words as they outline their teenager's presentation:

Attitude

Ronan and Nuala bring their sixteen-year-old son to see me. Parenting impulsive teenagers is a thankless task and the parents communicate how unimpressed they are as they witness how inconsiderate and selfish their child has become. As Lorcan plugs more into his peer world in new and exciting ways, he begins to care less about participation in family life. His 'to hell with it' attitude is impacting the harmony in their home. His attitude to school is concerning as he demonstrates disinterest and even contempt for school as grades slip and he starts getting into trouble with teachers. Their boy who was a model child, with excellent manners and always a pleasant demeanour, is now virtually unrecognisable. A new sarcastic tone is heard in his voice as backchat becomes a regular feature of interaction with his parents. As Nuala and Ronan describe this 'attitude problem' they are just so offended by how ungrateful their teenager is for all the sacrifices they make. They do so much for him, and he just throws it all back in their face. His parents are also upset and embarrassed by Lorcan's attitude towards the assessment meeting: slouching in his chair, rolling his eyes, shrugging his shoulders and failing to answer questions properly.

Respect

Nuala expresses her dismay at how rude and defiant her lovely little boy has become of late. He shows no respect when he talks to her and is so dismissive. His language is atrocious, and she doesn't know where he's picked it up, because he certainly doesn't hear it at home. Nuala can't ever imagine having spoken to her parents like that – she wouldn't have gotten away with it, but Lorcan seems to think that he can do what he likes. She suspects that his new friendship group, who are a bad influence, are beginning to rub off on Lorcan. When she asks him to do even the simplest of things, he rolls his eyes and argues back or goes to his room and closes the door behind him. It is as if her son has no respect for his parents or anyone else. Ronan agrees and adds that watching Lorcan treat them with such a lack of respect really bothers him. All they want is for their son to show them a bit of respect.

Trust

The parents then describe how they want to be able to trust their son but when they give him freedom or privilege Lorcan lets them down continually. He has broken their trust so many times and if they give him an inch, he takes a mile. He doesn't know when to stop and takes things too far. Lorcan has absolutely no sense of responsibility and they just can't trust him anymore. Recently, when Ronan and Nuala went away for the night, he pleaded with them to stay at home by himself instead of going to his grandparents' home. He assured them that he would have one friend over and would be responsible. Against their better judgement, they agreed. They were called at one o'clock in the morning by the police as Lorcan's house party had gotten out of hand. The parents had to come home. The adolescent seems to think it's OK that he can abuse his parents' trust at every turn. They were so disappointed that, at his age, he can't be trusted.

The assumptions and agendas for this assessment meeting, as with all initial encounters with impulsive teenagers and their parents, are predictable. Lorcan has zero interest in attending and sits with his head down and hood up. His expectation is that his parents will outline the litany of misdemeanours and I will set about putting manners on him. For Ronan and Nuala, they are relieved to be able to express their concerns to a professional and hope that I will take their wayward son in tow. After a handful of interventions to address the problem I will return him to them as a responsible, respectful mature son, student and citizen. As the therapist, my interest is twofold: offering understanding and attuned strategies to the parents so that their expectations for their son match his developmental location; and helping Lorcan to understand himself whilst nudging him along his path and towards more sophisticated developmental functioning.

Intuitive Parenting Strategies

Given the potential challenges faced by young people in today's world, it is understandable that parents are concerned at feeling locked out of their children's lives. However, this friction, which so often characterises the parent-adolescent relationship, is also partly due to the manner in which parents typically interact with their impulsive teenagers. For example, seven-year-old Jo's mother, Carol, picks her up from school and asks, *'How did your day go sweetie?'* There follows a fifteen-minute blow-by-blow account of the school day: what happened, what the teacher said, how playtime went, who was mean, how unruly the boys were and which of the girls is her new best friend today. When Carol asks what she'd like for dinner, they talk about all her favourite foods and she settles on a pasta dish. Jo loves her mother dearly and Carol feels like a great mother.

As the once-cherished relationship between parent and child is largely replaced by a defensive boundary, or on some days a formidable barricade, parents lament their loss of their lovely, kind child and try to figure out new ways of navigating life with a teenager who insists on shutting them out. Fast-forward a few years and Jo is now thirteen. Mum picks her up from school and asks, *'How did your day go sweetie?'* Jo answers, *'Fine.'* They're done. The conversation has ended for Jo. However, Carol is yearning for the closeness they once had and also wants to know what's happening in her daughter's life. So, she asks a second question, and a third. The conversation goes something like this:

Mum: *'How did you get on in school today?'*
Jo: *'Usual crap.'*
Mum: *'Now that's not a great attitude to have. Try to be positive.'*
Jo rolls her eyes, exasperated.
Mum: *'Did you have fun with your friends today?'*
Jo: *'I suppose.'*
Mum: *'What did you have for lunch?'*
Jo: *'I don't remember.'*
Mum: *'Have you much homework?'*
Jo: *'Aw, will you just stop talking about school.'*
Mum: *'Don't speak to me like that, there's no need to be rude Jo.'*
There follows a tense silence.
Mum: *'What would you like for dinner?'*
Jo: *'I dunno.'*
Mum: *'I'm stopping at the shop now. You need to tell me.'*
Jo: *'I'm not hungry.'*
Mum: *'Yeah, but you'll be hungry later.'*
Jo: *'Oh MY GOD will you just STOP?'*
Jo inserts her ear buds.

Carol has inadvertently and unwillingly found herself in the position of interrogator, having to drag conversation out of her daughter through a question-answer process. It is discouraging and unsatisfying for them both and soon they come to expect that their interactions will probably not end well. Jo finds her mother increasingly frustrating and Carol becomes more and more exasperated and, at times, infuriated. Contact has become non-receptive.

At this point, parents start to struggle. The parenting skill set which worked so well during the childhood years seems largely ineffective now: rules and limits are ignored; requests to undertake straightforward tasks turn into evening-long battles of wit; *because I said so* is met with a sarcastic *sure thing Mum*; and they don't so much ask if it's OK to have friends over as announce that it's happening. The intuitive approach to parenting younger children was relatively foolproof, however it no longer works, despite its remaining the most common mode of parenting impulsive teens. There are three elements to this intuitive parenting of impulsive teens strategy, which I also call the here's-what-not-to-do strategy:

Nagging

This is typically the first port of call for many parents – if at first you don't succeed, try, try, try, try, try and try again. It starts off as a tentative *suggestion* – *'Should you get that homework started?'* The parent doesn't hold out much realistic hope and they are right. Homework does not activate dopamine after all – unlike the constant hit received as teenagers scrolls through social media. After a few more robust suggestions, it intensifies to a *demand* and there is obvious frustration for both now: *'I'm sick telling you to get off that bloody phone and get that homework done. It's eight o'clock and you've been on it since you got home from school.'*

The likelihood of the homework getting started is even more remote now as the adolescent focuses not on the content of the demand, but rather on how annoying their parent is for interrupting their flow of dopamine with this insufferable badgering. Instead of thinking: *Mum's right; I should get to it now.* Their response is more likely to be: *'Would you just shut up and stop annoying me?'*…and if they don't say it out loud, they are almost certainly thinking it.

Impulsive adolescents will always attempt to reassure adults by communicating their intentions. *'I'll do in a while. I'll do it after this show.'* Smart parents don't buy it for a minute as the sweet draw of dopamine easily overcomes intention. With the failure of suggestion and now demand, their dialogue, which has maybe stretched over an entire evening, inevitably culminates in a *clash* with two unfolding scenarios:

> Either there is a shouting match with heated exchanges likely full of expletives and exaggerated language: *'You never listen to me; You're always on my back; You never do a damned thing I say; I get blamed for everything; You have no respect for me; You never take my side; You always have to have the last word.'*

Or the parent feigns detachment in an attempt to engender concern on the part of their teenager: *'Do you know what? I don't care anymore whether you do your damned homework or not. It can lie there. It's your own life and your own future you're throwing away. And don't come crying to me when you fail all your exams and you've nothing to show for your time in school. There's no good in being sorry then.'*

Nagging is an expression of powerlessness and the parent moves from mild irritation through to a posture of desperation where they try to coerce their adolescent into compliance via aggression or an if-you-don't-care-I-don't-care tactic, typically without success. Nagging rarely yields the desired results. Nightly homework battles between parents and teenagers are both vexatious and exhausting for all involved. The consequence of this cycle of *suggestion-demand-clash* is more likely to be a marked deterioration in the relationship between parent and teen.

Laundry is an ongoing and contentious issue in Bree's home where she and her teenage siblings are constantly nagged by their mother, Mary. The kids aren't particularly diligent about keeping their rooms tidy and Mary continually requests their cooperation: *'Would you for Heaven's sake put your dirty laundry in the baskets in your rooms so I don't have to pick it up off the floor?'*

This very reasonable request falls on deaf ears and Mary mostly ends up doing the laundry herself. Once it has been collected, washed, dried, ironed and folded, Mary sets neat piles for each of her teenage children on the steps of the stairs. She makes a request for them to lift their clean laundry pile and put it away next time they're going upstairs. However, each time Bree or her siblings climb the stairs they never quite feel like lifting the laundry piles. They'll do it next time. Inevitably someone inadvertently tips a pile all over the place and the teenagers continue to trample through the clothes, until eventually Mary brings them upstairs and puts them away herself.

'Is it too much to ask to keep your rooms tidy and help with the laundry? My back is broke traipsing after you bunch of ungrateful children. Do you think I've nothing better to do? I don't know why I bother.'

Bree finally works out that her mother is a gaslighting narcissist and besides, it was her mother's choice to have children. Bree didn't ask to be born. What did her mother expect?

Advice-giving

Without access to future-orientation and little evidence of personal accountability, parents feel the need to step in and attempt to instil some reason. Imparting the benefit of their wisdom to teenagers who don't share their caution and whose brains don't compute this way is an invitation for some eye-rolling:

'I'm just telling you this because I don't want you to make the same mistakes I made when I was your age... You need to put in the effort now and, trust me, you'll be glad in years to come that you worked hard at school and got your qualifications...I wish I had listened to my mother when I was young...There's a lot of pressure on young people your age to take drugs, but they're dangerous and you don't want to end up like your uncle Gerry...You drive far too fast, you need to slow down for you'll kill yourself or somebody else...Don't be sending pictures of yourself to boys, for once you send them you have no control who sees them...Behave yourself when you're out, you have your whole life ahead of you and don't ruin it by getting some girl pregnant.'

Of course, a gap in understanding renders this advice-giving redundant. No impulsive adolescent has ever expressed gratitude for parental advice: *'Thanks, Mum, for those words of wisdom, I'll integrate them into my considerations forthwith...'* is not the response typically uttered. Teenagers usually find advice from a parent either ridiculous, funny or both. I mean, what would a middle-aged person know about anything? The timing of this advice (which, it has to be said, is all very sound and very reasonable) is often problematic too. Parents tend to come in too quickly: Clara is telling her mother a hilarious story about two girls in her year who got so wasted having drinks whilst getting ready that they ended up not being able to go to the disco on Friday night. Her mother immediately runs in with caution and advice, pouring cold water over the story. What started off as a funny anecdote has evolved into a lecture on the demon drink. Clara regrets telling her mother, clams up and becomes frustrated. A potential moment of joining and positive influence has been compromised. There are ways to receive and respond to these stories but meeting them with advice is not one of them, if parents want to influence their teenagers to act responsibly. A little bite-your-tongue parenting is a good place to start.

Punishment and Threat

When all else fails, sanctions and bluster, usually laced with inconsistency, tend to fail too: *'If I catch you drinking again, you'll be grounded for the rest of the year… give me that phone until you have a bit of manners and then I'll give it back to you…if you don't tidy that bedroom right now, you're not going to the disco next week…if you can't behave yourself in this house then you can't have your friends over on Saturday.'*

An adolescent's response can range from being upset and huffing to fear or anger, right through to indifference. They sometimes care less about the consequence or know rightly that their parent won't carry the threat through. With an emphasis on maintaining influence over how their teenager conducts themselves, this authoritarian approach is usually an attempt to intimidate teenagers into being safer and taking more personal responsibility. The difficulty with this approach is that teenagers, like the rest of the world, tend not to flourish under threat. Instead, they may experience resentment, shame and further dislocation from parents.

It's Friday night and Lina's friends are at the youth club. However, she is sitting in her room alone and without her phone. It has been confiscated by her parents because it was discovered that she lied about where she was, who she was with and what she was doing the previous weekend. Her parents' hope is that she is upstairs reflecting on and willing to learn from her mistakes:

They're right, my behaviour last weekend was totally unacceptable and it's time I started becoming more responsible. Y'know, when I think about it, I get where my parents are coming from. I'm glad I've been given this time to consider the error of my ways. My parents really do have my best interests at heart. Yes, I'm annoyed that I didn't get to the youth club and that they took my phone away, but I appreciate their motivation in setting these consequences. My parents are the best!

The reality is more likely to be that Lina feels that the punishment is totally unreasonable, hates her parents even more and is in her room figuring out smarter ways of not getting caught next time – reinforcing her belief that she should hide things from her parents.

With their blatant disregard for others, especially parents, their lack of empathy, failure to consider the consequences of their actions, general irresponsibility and proneness to aggression, not to mention their inclination towards deceit and manipulation, raising adolescents when they are impulsively configured is generally not the highlight of a parent's experience. However, the developmental trajectory is towards increased connection between the limbic system and other functions such as emotional regulation, empathy and thinking things through. Impulsivity wanes and soon reasonable and mature human beings begin to emerge, to the relief and delight of parents everywhere.

Entrenched Impulsivity and Parenting

This is not the case when an adolescent shows signs of entrenched impulsivity, which is when the young person remains rigidly governed by limbic energy and does not progress in the anticipated developmental manner. In these instances, an intensely activated limbic system is ruling the roost, creating reactivity, dysregulation and all manner of chaos. These adolescents are drawn, in a more extreme manner than their developmentally impulsive counterparts, to seek pleasure which propels them towards risky behaviours. With entrenched impulsivity, the adolescent will characteristically demonstrate more extremely oppositional behaviour and the intuitive interventions of nagging, advice-giving and threats feel even more redundant for parents. In fact, young people are more likely to experience these as inflammatory and tensions can escalate. Emotional arousal is rapid and its intensity can resemble an explosion in a fireworks factory, with rages that can endure for hours at a time. Adolescents can be abusive to parents verbally, emotionally and physically, resulting in parents feeling intimidated and worried about their own and other family members' welfare.

Roisin cannot handle disruption to her dopamine flow and sometimes what seems like the simplest of things will set her off. When her parents attempt to impose a 10.30pm bedtime rule or remove her phone, she becomes extremely angry, shouts insults and throws things. Roisin is not moved by threats or bribes and simply walks out of the house when grounded. Her mother tries to reason with her, not understanding that attempting to do so with someone who is in an unreasonable frame of mind is both counterproductive and antagonistic. On occasion, these clashes between the pair spill over and Roisin shoves, pushes and hits her mum. Dad is incensed at this unacceptable behaviour and his responses inevitably inflame the situation even further. Roisin's parents have long ago reached the limits of their intuitive parenting skills and their strategies are ineffective. Over time the strongly limbic-activated adolescent's parents become mentally drained with the constant battles and the feeling that they have essentially no influence on their daughter's behaviour. Hopes that she would grow out of this impulsive presentation fade as adolescence progresses.

With unconstrained impulsivity, these teenagers cross a line that even the most high-spirited developmentally impulsive adolescent does not. Their level of dysregulation and persistent pushing of boundaries together with an inability to learn from previous experience often results in parents feeling that all of their approaches and interventions fall on deaf ears and are largely redundant. It is traumatic for parents rearing an adolescent who does not respond to reason, or to any parenting strategies, and whom a parent feels powerless to help. As well as a lot of 'bad parent' shame shuttling around, parents feel tremendously worried about what is to become of their child and how they will conduct themselves as adults. The parenting experience can be laced with disappointment and overwhelm when one is in constant battle with a teen's unchecked and surging limbic system. Parents tend not to be disappointed in their child, quite the opposite – they are filled with love and would lay down their lives for the sake of their teenager – but they feel it would have been so much easier for everyone, including and especially their child, if they had not been quite so impulsive.

Lorraine and Denise went to school together and have remained friends through the years. They both gave birth to children a few months apart and when they meet up, discuss their children's progress. Lorraine's daughter is good-natured and agreeable. She is academically capable and takes her studies seriously. She excels in extracurricular activities including music and sport and is now studying to become a teacher. Denise's son has been spirited and oppositional from early childhood and prone to tantrums which continue through the teenage years. He leaves school at the earliest opportunity and commitment to various types of work prove problematic. The adolescent parties all weekends and has developed an online gambling habit. His parents spend their time bailing him out financially and sorting out dramas, with no thanks and no sign of him mending the error of his ways. Denise becomes increasingly embarrassed and disheartened as she draws comparisons between the two teenagers. She feels bitter and jealous of Lorraine's experience of parenting which has all been relatively smooth sailing. Over time, Denise starts to compensate by fabricating success stories about her son, pretending that he is doing much better in the world than he is.

Parents can feel very lost and overwhelmed when entrenched impulsivity is organising their teenager's experience. Excessive and protracted impulsivity in relation to moods and behaviours typically creates issues at school and tends to mean that a child or adolescent's presentation warrants assessment for a psychiatric or neurodevelopment disorder. Engagement with various support systems can range from first-rate and transformational to unproductive and distressing. Parents dread the phone ringing during school hours as they come to assume it's yet another call from the vice-principal about their teenager's unacceptable behaviour and can sometimes feel judged or shamed in the face of a school's lack of understanding of the issue. With regard to adolescent mental health services, regrettably in today's world, well-intentioned professionals are working in overwhelmed and underfunded systems and attempts to access support can be unsatisfactory and demoralising.

Parents can feel isolated and alone, having little energy for anything else, as other children get overlooked and parental relationships become defined by the burden of managing the fallout of their adolescent's entrenched impulsivity. Struggles can surface as parents apply contrasting strategies to each crisis, resenting each other for the lack of support and understanding. For example, Paul and Anne disagree on the need for outside intervention. Paul feels that Anne mollycoddles and does everything for their son, which is half the problem. He downplays the extent of the issue: *'He's just doing what young lads do. Sure, I was like that myself when I was his age – doing a bit of wrecking and tearing round the country. He'll settle down soon enough.'*

Anne feels that Paul is utterly in denial of the gravity of the situation. She is mentally shattered and has begun to dislocate from her son, having tried nagging, bargaining, reasoning, aggression and bribery to no avail. *'I've washed my hands off him. He can go there, for I've had it with trying to get him to see sense. He doesn't give a damn about anything.'*

As we scratch beneath the surface, Anne is utterly broken-hearted for her and for her son and has collapsed under the weight of her exhaustion and sorrow.

Parenting adolescents who display entrenched impulsivity is unbelievably challenging and complex. It requires extraordinary patience and endurance, as well as intelligent, well-informed parenting strategies – and also often requires professional support. We will explore this in later chapters.

Chapter 8

Parenting the Inhibitive Adolescent

The greatest challenge when parenting inhibitive teens is the experience of power-lessness. As the cerebral cortex lights up with greater intensity and adolescents start thinking in a more self-referenced manner, an empathic posture, plenty of sensitivity and treading gently are called for. Teenagers feeling understood goes a long way towards helping them find balance and settling intense thoughts or emotions. However, many parents attempt to rescue and fix which isn't always well received. Trying to help is usually premature, unless adolescents first feel validated. Even so, a parent's advice which is both first-rate and rational can be ungraciously rebuffed. Patience, empathy and timing are required when negotiating life with a teenager who has a tendency to become self-absorbed. For parents, interaction with their teenager can feel baffling as they attempt to avoid stepping on landmines. This is partly due to the defensive nature of the inhibitive adolescent who will readily experience contact as critical and shaming. For example, Annie is getting ready to meet some friends. It is raining and she faces a twenty-minute walk into town. She texts her mum, *I wish I had my driving test and I could take the car in. I'll get soaked walking*. Her mum replies, *Why don't you take an umbrella with you and it'll keep you dry?* Annie's response is *Fuck off*. When we unpack this interaction, Annie believes that her mother was having a dig at her for not getting around to applying for her provisional driver's licence. Her mum was simply trying to be helpful.

Or Maya, who has just been dumped by her boyfriend. The adolescent is more connected with the *idea* of being in a relationship with Ben than whether or not they are a good fit. He is attractive and much sought after, but really quite dull and annoying. Still, the relationship elevates her peer status, which is important to Maya. After a number of months, rumours start to circulate on social media about Ben's connection with a girl in the year below Maya. A short time later, he ends their romance and starts dating this younger girl. The rejection feels like public humiliation and the adolescent is convinced she is a laughingstock among her peers. Added to this, Maya's heart starts to open to Ben: now that she can't have him, he is all she wants. This infatuation for her ex-boyfriend, much like the original relationship, is much more a statement about Maya's self-perception and need for validation than it is about Ben. The adolescent opens up on a long car journey to

DOI: 10.4324/9781003373599-11

her mother, as teenagers are inclined to do, and shares her distress. Maya's mother encourages her to look on the bright side, reminding her daughter that she is beautiful and that there are plenty of fish in the sea. Her mum also shares that she is a little relieved, as she didn't really think Ben was a suitable boyfriend for Maya. The adolescent responds, *'Just stop talking, you don't even understand. I wish I hadn't said anything.'* Maya's mother bites back that she was only trying to help. The pair drive on in silence – the adolescent appalled at her mother's insensitivity.

Inhibitive adolescents have an acute yearning to be understood, which is why self-reflection, poetry and falling in love appeal at this stage. They are venturing into deeper dimensions of the self and it can all feel a little isolating and unsteadying. Parents can unwittingly make situations worse during interactions with worked-up teenagers. Reasoning with an adolescent whose configuration style is inhibitive can result in parents being scorned. This is because adolescents who are inhibitively configured struggle to see the bigger picture or develop a more realistic view of situations. It will take a little while for them to find more solid ground and greater personal stability.

Whilst the majority of adolescents weave in and out of intense self-process through the adolescent years, plenty struggle with deep-seated and persistent anxiety which holds them captive in a constant loop of self-referenced negativity. Rather than momentary wobbles and dramas, this more entrenched inhibitive configuration style defines the entire lifespace and prevents young people from fully living their lives. Rearing a very anxious adolescent presents additional challenges for parents whose dilemma is how to inspire self-belief and liberate their teenagers from overthinking their way through the world. This can feel like an impossible task.

Parenting Inside the Comfort Zone

The opposite of anxiety is courage and if adolescents were to listen to their anxiety all the time, they would avoid many of life's situations. For example, public speaking will generate anxiety for many. Part of them is scared of messing up, looking nervous and sounding dumb...and yet, another part would love to do it and knows they'll be really glad they did. Hopefully, by the time the presentation comes around, most of the adolescent's anxiety will have morphed into excitement and determination. Entrenched inhibitive adolescents, however, struggle more than most in these, and even in the most innocuous, situations. Caustic self-dialogue reminds them how worthless they are and focuses on negativity and failure. It is difficult for adolescents to take risks when they convince themselves that they are not good enough, lack self-confidence, live in fear and restrict their lifespace. It is equally painful for parents who feel powerless to intervene. Despite investing so much time and love in building their teenage children up, very little seems to work, as anxiety and restriction become entrenched.

In the spirit of support and confidence-building, parents can inadvertently validate the externalised sense of self, where acceptance is sought from performance, image and outward symbols of success. Rachel excels in academics and sport. Her parents are so proud of how she works so hard and is so driven. She puts great effort into everything that she does, and their sense of pride is obvious. As a top student and captain of the sports team, Rachel's parents are delighted that their daughter is so successful. Academics and qualifications are emphasised in the family culture and Rachel is more than reaching the bar. Every time she passes another exam or wins another trophy, her parents delight in her achievements and more praised is heaped on Rachel. A bright future lies ahead, for sure. However, when anxiety symptoms threaten to derail her senior exams, the adolescent's parents bring her to see me. As I ask her father to give a general description of his daughter as a person. He states:

'Rachel is just amazing. She is so committed to her schoolwork and her football and works extremely hard. We could not be more proud of her.'

There isn't much more to say, apart from describing her anxiety symptoms. Her mother's description is along the same lines. I wonder how the adolescent might hear this – I have invited her parents to outline their daughter's nature and they both respond by commending her perfectionist tendencies and her achievements. Rachel's parents love her deeply and are desperately trying to instil positivity and self-belief in their daughter. However, during a one-to-one meeting with me, the adolescent reveals that she experiences her parents' encouragement as both the only way to feel validated by them and as pressure to not let them down. Parental pride and praise are unintentionally feeding into Rachel's externalised sense of self. Her well-intentioned parents do not perceive that her driven nature and extremely high expectations of herself are symptoms of a deeper discomfort within herself which they themselves are fostering.

As university and leaving home are now on the horizon, the biggest hurdle for the adolescent is the academic pressure she applies to herself and the tsunami of stress which overtakes her during the exam period. By the time her anxiety symptoms are at problematic levels, dialogue between Rachel and her parents focuses on two principal issues – her successes and her symptoms.

The relationships which entrenched inhibitive adolescents have with people inside their comfort zone tend to be characterised by dependency. Being overly reliant on a parent means that there is a closeness between the two. As the young person looks to a parent for support, they learn to grow dependent on that parent to provide the emotional and psychological comfort and security which they themselves find difficult to create. Comfort parents are a great source of oxytocin, a comfort hormone. A reciprocal dynamic is often at play here too, where certain parents like being turned to for support.

Agnieska's mother Katarzyna is part of her daughter's comfort zone. They enjoy spending time in each other's company and Katarzyna regularly organises activities from the pair to do, as Agnieska struggles with peer friendships. Agnieska's social life amounts to shopping and cinema trips with her mother. Katarzyna is upset that her daughter doesn't have any close friends. The adolescent seems willing to tolerate peripheral friendship – being on the sidelines and included when other girls feel like it – though not being invited to activities outside school. Despite it creating considerable distress for Agnieska, she also doesn't want to rock the boat and momentary belonging appears to be worth the pain. Katarzyna encourages her daughter to ditch these girls and find some good friends. She is baffled when her daughter refuses even to consider this advice, as Agnieska appears almost grateful for the morsels of friendliness afforded her. Katarzyna coaches her daughter about standing up for herself and what to say to these girls, overlooking the reality that Agnieska is not assertive and cannot find her voice in the most straightforward of situations, never mind challenging peers who matter to her. This cycle of Agnieska expressing her dissatisfaction and upset at how she is being treated, her mother arming her with strategies to move on and make new friends, followed by the teenager closing down, is a very regular feature of their conversations.

Inhibitive adolescents tend not to embrace risk or the unfamiliar. They appreciate the relief and respite afforded to them by the people, places and things which constitute their comfort zone. The forbidden activity associated with their impulsive counterparts tends not to be a problem – they are not out getting drunk or smoking weed, and partying is not usually a concern. On the contrary, rather than creating boundaries with parents, many inhibitive adolescents share a good deal of their private experience with parents and involve them in their day to day living. Inhibitive adolescents, by and large, prefer their parents to be close by. For example, the Friday night disco is the single most important event in Oscar's week. The dopamine is flowing for this impulsive adolescent who is fired up with excitement, planning the evening with friends, organising fake ID, getting alcohol and hoping to get lucky with the girl he likes. Conversely, Chloe, an entrenched inhibitive adolescent, prefers to stay home and watch a favourite childhood movie snuggled with her parents and younger siblings, eating popcorn. The disco feels too threatening – putting on a dress and looking terrible compared to the beautiful people who will be there, talking to people, everyone watching and judging as she dances, knowing people will be drinking and terrified that someone might ask her out – not to mention the fact that she will be separated from the safety and ease of her comfort zone.

The first stage in the development of a strong, healthy sense of self which unfolds in adolescence does not happen for these inhibitive adolescents. Reluctance to leave the comfort zone thwarts these initial attempts at developing a sense of self. The process of boundarying the world of childhood (because it's so immature and uncool) and boundarying of the adult world (because they are insufferable and forever on teenagers' backs) in order to find a place of belonging within the peer landscape is bypassed. The result tends to be an adolescent who is intellectually advancing, but who remains emotionally, socially and psychologically immature.

Parenting at The Edge of the Comfort Zone

Though they may try desperately, it is not possible for adolescents to constantly remain within the confines of their comfort zone. Life transpires to create evolution and flux, though without the resources of courage and faith in themselves or the world, this shifting is perceived as threatening and anxiety-inducing. When inhibitive adolescents are presented with situations outside the comfort zone, this creates emotional and psychological instability. In fact, the mere thought of these things, such as going to school or interacting in a group, is nearly always worse than the actual situations themselves. This brings them to the edge of the comfort zone, where adolescents spend a great deal of time obsessively worried, overthinking, preoccupied and feeling very anxious. Dialogue with parents at the edge of the comfort zone tends to focus on the threat from outside, for example, belonging with peers, interacting with people, schoolwork and grades, body image, sporting performance, the future, people dying, readiness to leave home for college and not being good enough. Parents do their best to ease their teenager's anxiety and calm the insecure, neurotic thoughts. However, they quickly become aware that they are able to do very little to alleviate these, often ungrounded, fears and anxieties.

Anxiety is contagious and as adolescents express their unease and apprehension, parents tend to feel anxious and overwhelmed themselves. Witnessing their children being flooded with an inhibitive mindset of relentless overthinking, a hostile self-perception and lack of courage to push out into the world, parents feel deep despair. Experiencing themselves as essentially powerless while they watch their beloved children becoming consumed with dread is a very unsettling experience for any parent. They feel the need to do *something* and often intuitive parenting strategies are employed with limited, if any, longer-term success.

The Reassuring Parent

Reassuring is by far the most common approach to parenting adolescents whose configuration style is inhibitive – and reassuring parents tends to be recruited into the comfort zone. As the young person expresses their worries and fears, and describes their anxiety symptoms, parents attempt to soothe them by explaining why they shouldn't think and feel the way they do. *'There's no need to be worried; nothing bad is going to happen; try not to think about it; you'll be absolutely fine; why don't you just focus on positive thoughts.'*

Whilst reassuring conversations may help in the moment, as soon as the reassuring stops, the pressure starts again. Imagine you receive a large bill you don't have the money to pay and you share this with your friend. They might say: *'Don't worry yourself about it, the money will come from somewhere, it always does. And sure, there are worse things to worry about. It's only money for goodness' sake. Trust the universe to provide.'* That's certainly reassuring to hear *in the moment* but as soon as the conversation is over, the dread in the pit of your stomach, the waves of fear and the mental preoccupation come back in full force. It's the same with trying to reassure an anxious adolescent. Reassurance works momentarily for the teenager and supports the parent to feel that they are actually doing something useful, however the same recycling dialogue takes place on a regular basis – sometimes several times a day. The problem with this approach is that the comfort is short-lived, and the strategies usually do not resolve anxiety. Nonetheless, the time spent in reassuring dialogue can be considerable and it is not uncommon for concerns regarding the inhibitive adolescent to monopolise a parent's time and headspace.

Darren's mother, Caroline, is his greatest comfort. He struggles being away from her and becomes upset if an occasional night out has been arranged with family or friends. When his mother is at home, he feels safe, happy and confident…but his world is filled with insecurity and terror when she leaves. Caroline had hoped that he would grow out of this as a teenager, however Darren continues to experience high anxiety when she is away from the comfort zone. Flooded with anxiety, Darren typically sends dozens of texts and calls her every few minutes during a night out – describing how anxious he feels, telling her how much he misses her, making sure she is OK and pleading with her to come home soon. As a result, Caroline rarely goes out.

Parents tend to creatively adjust by restricting activities and all members of the family can feel held hostage to an adolescent's entrenched inhibitive configuration style. Darren much prefers to be in the comfort of home, pottering around with his mother present. He likes to be in his bedroom on screens and doesn't actually spend much time with her directly – just so long as she is in close proximity. He also doesn't care much about where other family members are as they are not a particular source of comfort. Eating out in restaurants, trips to the cinema, weekend breaks and summer holidays are part of the family culture which the adolescent's parents have envisaged. However, from childhood Darren has demonstrated discomfort and distress when participating in anything which involves novelty, flexibility and change. As a result, the family have never enjoyed these experiences, and everyone misses out because Darren finds it difficult to cope in these situations. The parents endure an ongoing dilemma of trying to balance not wanting to overwhelm their anxious son with creating enriching experiences for their family as a whole. The adolescent's anxiety usually wins out.

The Enabling Parent

It is very distressing for parents to watch their adolescent struggle relentlessly. On school mornings there are tears, panic attacks, meltdowns and descriptions of how much they hate their lives. Some parents make the call not to make their teenage children endure this anguish. Patterns of not trying to overcome anxious experience are established as staying within the limits of what feels comfortable becomes the culture. One of the tasks of parenting is about getting the balance right between support and challenge. However, there is little by way of challenge in these situations. The parent tends to do everything for their teenager and does not encourage expansion of the lifespace.

Martina's daughter Riley finds school overwhelming. Every morning is an ordeal and on the days Riley goes in, this commonly ends in a phone call to her mother late morning to come pick her up. Martina finds it heart-breaking to bear witness to her daughter's suffering and resolves not to put her through it any longer. She now asks her daughter if she is going to school the next day. Riley says *'no'* and that is that. When challenged by education professionals about the adolescent's poor attendance, Martina feels frustrated and resentful that she is being held to account. These people have no idea how difficult it is for her daughter to attend school. Whilst it is understandable that Martina does not want Riley to suffer distressing fear and anxiety, the adolescent's reliance on the comfort zone becomes even more entrenched. The teenager sleeps until noon and sit in her pyjamas for the rest of her day on screens. When she wants something, her mother gets it for her. When she needs to go somewhere, her mother accompanies her or goes for her. Riley becomes increasingly dependent on her comforting parent and the possibility of living a full life out in the world seems more and more remote. Martina feels powerless to do anything about the situation.

The Discomforting Parent

If a parent does not add to the adolescent's need for comfort, then they are relegated by the young person to outside the comfort zone. This parent may adopt a no-nonsense approach to an excessively inhibitive presentation, hoping that the young person will 'snap out of it' and stop this senseless behaviour. They can become frustrated when their efforts are predictably rebuffed. Cora is reluctant to go to school. Her father orders her to get her bag and get out to the car, which makes her even more upset. As they reach the school gates her appeals to her dad are lost on him. He speaks firmly to her: *'Come on now, stop this nonsense. If your younger sister can do it, you can do it. Don't be a baby…there's no need for these tears. Stop crying, get out of the car and get into school.'*

The discomforting parent may also be emotionally distant and uncomfortable talking about the young person's feeling world. Cora is very close with her mother but would never dream of talking to her father about her struggles and he would never dream of enquiring. She is loath to have him involved in her life much at all, preferring her mother to be present or bring her places. Cora's discomfort with her father has become so heightened that she finds it difficult to cope with the sound of him chewing or breathing. In the extreme, the discomforting parent's presence cannot be tolerated at all, as adolescents become phobic around the parent. Gradually Cora dreads when her father is home. She feels at ease with her mother and siblings, though finds it impossible to be around him. Everything he does now infuriates her and her relationship with him is characterised by avoidance and contempt.

The adolescent refuses to be in the same room with him and if he tries to talk with her, she shuts down. Family life becomes very tense and stressful for everyone as they navigate this phobic alienation.

When the adolescent experiences one parent as discomforting, the result is greater reliance on and closeness with the parent who has been recruited into the comfort zone. However, their closeness is infused with the adolescent's dependency and need for comfort. As Cora feels soothed only by her mother, confides in this one parent alone and feels more secure when mum is around, it can be both pressuring and endorsing for the comfort parent. It can feel like a great compliment for parents when they have such a close relationship with their adolescent. This commonly impacts the parental relationship, as conflicting parenting strategies create tension. I often encounter situations where the comforting parent has more of a relationship with their inhibitive teenager than with their partner. If the young person is living with parental separation, an additional complexity may be the adolescent's reluctance to spend time with a non-comforting parent. The adolescent objects to leaving the familiarity of their comfort zone – the parent, their bedroom, their routines.

Alienation of Both Parents

In some situations, the adolescent seeks comfort from neither parent. They keep both at arm's length and suffer in silence. Their comfort zone is populated with screens, sports and other interests. There may be some social interaction with peers, however parents are not welcome. This is a very powerless position for parents who are unable to help or support their teenager due to being expelled from the comfort zone. Seventeen-year-old Olly manages to attend school, though finds it very pressure-inducing. As his senior exams approach, without consultation with either parent or anyone from the adult world, he announces that he is dropping out of school. His daily routine becomes disorganised and he sits up for most of the night and sleeps during the day until early evening. Olly's parents watch him struggle throughout his adolescence, trying to manage an increasingly stressful lifespace. They witness how his social anxiety, academic stress and lack of confidence create increasing hardship and overwhelm for him. However, Olly shuts them out and refuses to engage with them or accept support in relation to any aspect of his struggles. In fact, the adolescent responds with overt hostility when his parents reach out. This is heart-breaking for his parents who are beside themselves with worry.

Eggshell Parenting

As mentioned previously, some adolescents – particularly boys – tend to hold their anxiety privately and with intensity in the world, then express it as frustration at home. A good deal of eggshell parenting happens when living with anxious adolescents, particularly those who keep their parents at a distance and are unwilling to accept support. As the young person moves from relative calm into some level of stress, their agitation grows. Parents can easily recognise this shift. Patricia picks her son up from school every afternoon:

'I know as soon as I see him coming out of school what type of evening we're going to have. If he's had a bad day, the head will be down, he'll get into the car and not speak, and I can't say anything right. I've learned to keep my mouth shut and say nothing. Then when we get home, the whole atmosphere in the house changes. I'm trying to keep everyone from upsetting him, but somewhere along the line there's going to be a scene.'

These are difficult situations for parents who want to help but are pushed away as the adolescent's private world of inner experience remains off-limits. Parental intervention is an important first step when offering support in these situations where there is alienation and eggshelling, as parents tend to feel utterly powerless to influence their adolescents.

Limiting of Parental Support

Sixteen-year-old Yvonne experiences entrenched inhibition and compensates for her perceived inadequacy and low self-worth by becoming a perfectionist, driving herself to achieve. She is highly competitive and excels academically, musically and in sport. Never good enough, she becomes more and more preoccupied with her weight. Yvonne begins applying increasing restrictions to her diet whilst pushing herself harder when running. Her overthinking leads to a rigid fixation about all things related to body shape, food and exercise. The adolescent's uncompromising determination leads her into the territory of an eating disorder. Following a diagnosis of anorexia, Yvonne's parents berate themselves for not having realised the extent of the problem sooner. They are shocked and wonder to themselves how they could have let this happen. As mealtimes loom or Yvonne prepares to go for a run, parental stress levels surge. Whilst the adolescent experiences their attempts to support as intrusive, Yvonne's parents feel excluded and unable to influence their daughter's diet and exercise regimes. They watch on helplessly as their daughter drives herself to greater extremes. Yvonne feels intensely scrutinised by parents and professionals. The adolescent's mother and father feel they are failing as parents, and as their guilt grows stronger so does their exhaustion. The family become more insular as parents do not wish to talk about their daughter's struggles with wider family and friends. Yvonne's parents grow as preoccupied with the adolescent's mindset and behaviours as she is. Dialogue seems to focus almost exclusively on the eating disorder as well as Yvonne's academic, music and sporting performance. The adolescent continues to enjoy a relatively close, supportive relationship with her parents – except when they introduce any dialogue related to anorexia. In these moments, she reacts defensively and often with hostility.

Gender Discomfort

Some adolescents who demonstrate an entrenched inhibitive configuration style experience discomfort in relation to their gender assignment, which can create dilemmas for parents. Whilst some parents readily embrace their teenager's experience and support the direction in which the young person wishes to move with regards to gender identity and expression, others struggle greatly. When Des shares that they identify as non-binary and request that parents use they/them pronouns going forward, their parents, Claire and James are taken aback, to put it mildly. As the adolescent's experience of gender evolves, she identifies as transgender. During further conversations with her parents, the teenager confirms that she identifies wholly as a girl, has opted to change her name to Natalie and wishes to pursue hormone therapy with urgency. On hearing this, Claire sheds many tears and feels heartbroken much of the time – for both herself and her child. She tries to be accepting but finds it all so difficult. The adolescent's dad James dismisses it as the influence of social media and figures that his son is likely copying a fad: people have been putting ideas in his head. This teenage nonsense will recede in time and doesn't need to be taken particularly seriously.

Meanwhile for Natalie, the idea of living as a boy and inhabiting the male form creates considerable distress and the adolescent has begun to self-harm. Natalie's ultimate goal is to have feminising surgery and live fully as a female. The parents feel that they no longer know or understand their child and are completely out of their depth in this new terrain. They can't comprehend how someone would feel this way – the concept is utterly alien to them and certainly not something they had anticipated as they prepared themselves for parenting their teenager. For Claire and James, the idea of their lovely son inviting so much disruption and potential adversity into his life seems senseless. Claire manages to refer to the teenager as Natalie in her presence, though still thinks of her as Des, her beloved son. She feels traumatised by not being able to access Des: framed childhood photographs have been removed from walls and Natalie becomes agitated when her previous identity as a boy is mentioned. Getting pronouns wrong feels like stepping on a landmine. James, the adolescent's father, resists adjusting and simply avoids calling his child by any name when in Natalie's presence. He struggles to get his head round any of it.

Raising an entrenched inhibitive, characteristically anxious teenager is demanding for parents. Adolescents may dread school, struggle with relationships and isolation, remain inflexible and demonstrate unhealthy levels of dependency on parents. At the same time, they may prove themselves to be highly capable and driven, achieving great success. Parents get caught in this dichotomy and apply intuitive approaches to tackling anxiety: reassuring and encouraging where there is self-doubt and celebrating external accomplishments. However, very little seems to work. Ubiquitous pressure leaves the adolescent feeling wired with stress, creating an ongoing need for decompression within the comfort zone. Parents, in turn, feel overwhelmed and anxious themselves – hating to see their children so distressed. To make matters worse, it can be a challenge to source professional support these days which can ramp up parents' experience of powerlessness and isolation. Parental burnout is common and, quite often, I find that parents are as worn out as their adolescents by the time they reach my office.

Chapter 9

Parenting the Directional Adolescent

A common trajectory for parents is initially to spend considerable time concerned about their teenager's attitude, lack of respect and continual breaching of trust with adults. Parenting strategies might include nagging, lecturing and grounding their children during these earlier years of adolescence in an attempt to influence their teenagers to knuckle down and apply themselves to school, be considerate and helpful around the house, stop hanging out with bad-influence friends and not take irresponsible risks, such as getting drunk or high or compromising themselves sexually. This may then be followed by a period spent eggshelling around intense and self-conscious adolescents in the throes of existential angst. Parenting strategies tend to include reassuring and varying degrees of response to their teenager's highly self-conscious appraisal – from attuned empathy to unsympathetic dismissal. As inhibitive teenagers struggle to feel understood, parents often try to make their teenager feel better, but in doing so, inadvertently end up making things worse.

It is a welcome relief when frontal lobe activation becomes figural and the days of concentrated supervision of impetuous teens or the soothing of narcissistic rumination about appearance, grades, what everyone thinks of them, finally start to wane. As adolescents become increasingly directional, they grow more emotionally stable. The development of psychological balance creates a more positive self-image and courageous worldview, as adolescents exert greater independent management over their lives. Self-acceptance organically extends to greater acceptance of others as directional adolescents develop the capacity for empathy and mutual consideration. *Finally*, they see parents as decent, reasonable human beings again and life becomes a little more relaxed. Frontal lobe-activated adolescents require minimal parental intervention and conversations between them now take on more of a consultative, mutual quality. They ask for advice from parents – even taking it on board – and are appreciative for the most part.

Twenty-two-year-old Alanna has attained a level of resilience with regards to selfhood and as a result of this she stands on more solid ground within herself. Her contact with the adult world becomes more mature. The adolescent is a great help around the house and always even-keeled. If a parent asks her to do something, she doesn't need to be told twice. Gone are the days of asking a parent's permission to

DOI: 10.4324/9781003373599-12

go out and Alanna takes responsibility to manage much of her day-to-day life. She is friendly and open with her parents and no longer sees them as obstructions to her happiness or just there to bail her out. Her need for parental input amounts to consultative dialogue about various dimensions of her lifespace. Right now, she's figuring out whether she should apply for a Master's study programme immediately after she completes her undergraduate degree, or whether she should spend a year in Australia first. Whilst weighing up her options, she engages her parents in conversation – curious to hear their points of view and open to accepting their advice. Alanna doesn't feel that her parents are bossing her around and telling her what to do. She doesn't feel the need to ask their permission. The adolescent isn't collapsing with indecision and needing to be rescued by her parents. Alanna has the measure of herself, is considering her options with self-possessed insight and is simply using the dialogue with her parents as a sounding board to support greater clarity. At the end of the day, this is her life and she will make the final call about the best way forward. Whilst her parents may still worry about her, they trust her as she steps out into the world. Parenting for Alanna's mother and father is relatively smooth and uncomplicated. They trust she is able to handle herself for the most part and that when she is not, she will reach out for support.

Directional adolescents are responsive to intuitive parenting strategies, which is a welcome turn of events, particularly if there are also impulsive and inhibitive teens in the house. And as mentioned previously, some adolescents are directional throughout their teenage years – with access to the integrating functions of the frontal lobe – wobbling here and there but moving in the right direction for the most part. They will weave in and out of episodes of impulsivity and inhibition, but not remain there for very long. They are responsive, respectful, level-headed, considered and parenting these adolescents is a dream. These teenagers are *great*, *obliging* and they *just get on with it*. Their parents are generally not banging down the doors of therapists' offices looking for advice and strategies. When parenting directional adolescents, people feel like good parents and it's relatively smooth sailing.

Multiple Parenting Strategies

With three very distinct configuration styles in adolescence - impulsive, inhibitive and directional – three different levels of parenting strategy are required. The one-size-fits-all approach, which may have been effective in previous generations, certainly will not work in today's Western culture. Intuitive parenting strategies involve reasoning and they make a great deal of sense. These are suited for directional adolescents who have developed some capacity to contain their emotions and apply bigger-picture thinking to any issues they may have. The drama of earlier adolescent process is replaced with increased stability and calm. So, when parents appeal through reasoning, directional adolescents are usually open to and able to take this on board. However, they have their limitations as parents draw a blank when applying these strategies to their impulsive and inhibitive teenage children.

As adolescents don't come with a troubleshooting guide, innate, in-built parenting strategies which are perfectly reasonable and applicable to the more directional young people tend to backfire when parents are attempting to influence a feelings-dominated (impulsive) or cognitively imbalanced (inhibitive) teenager. Mothers and fathers grow weary of the regular showdowns, battles of will and constant monitoring which become the defining features of life with impulsive adolescents; or the non-stop reassuring, rescuing and dependency which characterises life with inhibitive adolescents. In these situations, parenting can become entrenched, powerless and disheartening.

For example, Tina has three teenage children, Kayden, Zoe and Ruth. It's half past ten on a school night and time for bed. The kids are all in their bedrooms on screens. Kayden is limbic-activated and enjoying the banter and competition with friends on his game console. He responds to his mother's request with a look of desolation in his eyes and a plea to stay online just until he finishes this one game. This is a very important game. To exit early would be disastrous and besides, he's not even tired. Twenty minutes later and Kayden hasn't budged. There is some nagging, a mini-lecture about improving his attitude and the importance of sleep for mental health, followed by Tina threatening not to let him out at the weekend. Kayden doesn't care whether she does or not – he just really cares about the fun he's having *now*. The stand-off finally ends in a shouting match with Kayden huffing and puffing around his bedroom, reluctantly getting ready for bed. He continues to protest about being treated unfairly and how his mother never makes the other two go to bed. *Why does she always pick on him?* To add insult to injury, he's the *only* person in his class who is made to go to bed at this utterly unreasonable time of the day. *Everyone else* is allowed to stay up to whatever time they want. Tina worries about Kayden's attitude.

Zoe is inhibitive and governed by a still-developing cerebral cortex, meaning that she feels insecure and anxious a good deal of the time. She has been studying for hours, doing some coursework and organising her notes. When Tina lets her know it's time for bed, Zoe tells her that she has homework still to complete. There are just not enough hours in the day for all the work she needs to do. The adolescent expresses her worry that she has so much to do, with exam season rapidly approaching. She shares her fears with Tina about not being able to sleep again tonight due to overthinking about her college application process – due in eighteen months. As she mentions this, a conversation ensues in which she reviews her options for the umpteenth time, laments her indecisiveness and worries that she probably won't be accepted for any of the courses she might apply for. Tina reassures her that she's worked so hard, is so smart and whatever course she chooses will work out just fine. As Zoe starts to get ready for bed an hour later, she gets panicky at the thought of school tomorrow and reaches out for her mother's comfort and reassurance. Tina worries about the amount of pressure her daughter puts on herself.

Ruth, the directional adolescent, has completed what needed to be done for her homework earlier and is on her phone. Tina pops her head around Ruth's bedroom door.

Mum: *'Time for bed Ruth.'*
Ruth: *'OK Mum, goodnight.'*

Ruth, who is directional, turns her notifications off and puts her phone away (because getting an uninterrupted night's sleep is important to her), goes straight to the bathroom to brush her teeth and is in bed within twenty minutes. No protesting, no drama, just doing what Tina asks because she sees that mum has enough on her plate managing the two younger siblings. Ruth would quite like to sit on her phone for another while but gets that doing so will leave her tired the next morning, so she applies discipline to her impulse. The adolescent has faith that she is adequately prepared for school the next day so there is no need to give it another thought. No counterproductive rumination required. Tina thinks to herself what a great child Ruth is. *Why couldn't the other two be more like Ruth?*

Next morning, Ruth's alarm clock goes off and up she gets. Meanwhile there's another shouting match trying to get Kayden up for school. He can't get out of bed because he's so tired, which generates more nagging and a lecture to the tune of *if you would go to bed when you're told instead of sitting on that bloody Xbox half the night.* Zoe is tearfully upset about going to school and has a panic attack, which necessitates a phone call to the school and Tina being late for work. She eventually drives Zoe in at 9.45am. It's not fair that she gets to go into school late and Kayden is always made to go in even on days that he's sick. She never believes him, and Zoe always gets away with *everything.*

With a directional configuration style, Ruth is an easy person to parent because she is relatively emotionally stable, responds to reason and takes ownership of her lifespace. As directional adolescents are naturally prone to do, Ruth 'just gets on with it'. She is considerate of her parent and can see things from mum's perspective. Ruth is aware of how demanding her mother's life can be. One evening, her mother looks exhausted. Anxious Zoe notices this and despite feeling very guilty about burdening her mother, does so anyway. Her need to experience some comfort and reassurance takes precedence. That same evening, Kayden lets his mother know that because he forgot his geography book, he has to borrow his friend's one (the teacher has threatened him with a week's detention if he fails to hand in his work again). Mum will have to drive him over to collect it – a sixteen-mile round trip – and this has to happen before his football training, which she also has to run him to and pick him up from afterwards. Also…he quite fancies a pizza for tea – the nice ones from that place in the next town. Ruth, his directional, considerate older sister tells Kayden that mum is tired and asks him not to place so many demands on her time and energy. Kayden responds, *'…but that's her job!'* Ruth does what she can that evening to help out – not because she particularly wants to, but because she sees that her mother could do with some support and so it's the right thing to do.

Tina treats her three teenage children equally…or so she thinks. She will say that she does not have a favourite child and loves them all the same. Her children may disagree. Everyone knows that Zoe is spoiled and gets special treatment; Kayden gets a hard time and is always in trouble; and Ruth is her favourite. Whilst Tina is convinced that she makes no differences between the three, imperceptibly to her, there are nuances in her contact which affect the quality of relating. These subtleties shape not only what happens in each of the parent-teenager relationships but also influence how each adolescent thinks of themselves. These are evident when mum is talking to or about her children.

Let's say the Kayden, Zoe and Ruth arrive home from school off the bus. Kayden comes through the door first:

Mum:	*'Well…how did you get on today?'*
Kayden:	*'Fine.'*
Mum:	*'What did Mr McGuigan say about not having your project done?'*
Kayden:	*'Nothing.'*
Mum:	*'You'll need to get that done this evening. There'll be no playing that Xbox and messing about like you usually do.'*
Kayden:	*'Aw, do I have to? He'll not even look at it anyway. He literally doesn't care.'*
Mum:	*'You're doing it and that's final. This is your big year. You're going to have to buck up your attitude.'*

Kayden tuts, rolls his eyes and sighs.

Mum:	*'Do you have any other homework tonight?'*
Kayden:	*'No.'*
Mum:	*'Let me see that homework diary.'*

Micro-aggressions in both Tina's body language and dialogue with Kayden are apparent. She places her hands on her hips and adopts a mildly aggressive, suspicious tone. Her subconscious message to her son is: *I see you and the first thing I consider is that there's likely to have been some trouble today. Here's how this evening is going to work: I'm going to lay down the law authoritatively though we both know that you won't listen. You're not to be trusted. I don't take you seriously and I don't expect that you will take yourself seriously.* Tina knows her son and she's right to be suspicious. He probably did get into trouble today, has no intention of completing his project and is very likely lying about not having homework to do. Kayden feels constantly criticised and chastised. His mother is always on his back which is why he is usually armed and guarded for the onslaught that's coming his way when Tina and he are together. Tina's reliance on her intuitive parenting strategies of nagging, lecturing and punishing create shame in their relating and drive a wedge between them.

Zoe comes in next.

Mum:	*'Darling, how did you get on today pet?'*
Zoe:	*'Really bad.'*
Mum:	*'Oh sweetheart. Let me give you a big hug.'*

Zoe: *'I couldn't stay in geography class, I felt claustrophobic and could hardly breathe.'*

Mum: *'You're home now. Try not to think about it anymore. You did your best.'*

Zoe: *'I am so tired, and I have so much homework to do.'*

Mum: *'Why don't you go upstairs and change out of your uniform? I'll bring you up a hot chocolate and we can chat it through.'*

Knowing how much her daughter struggled to attend school today, with so much anxiety and having slept poorly the night before, her mother's demeanour softens. She tilts her head to the side and adopts a sympathetic tone. Tina knows that Zoe will need her mother's time and reassurance to let go of today, manage homework stress and prepare for having to do it all again tomorrow. Mum's subtle message to Zoe is: *I don't anticipate that today will have gone well for you. I don't have faith in you, and I don't expect that you will have faith in yourself.*

Ruth comes in last.

Ruth: *'Hi Mum.'*

Mum: *'Hi Ruth. How did you get on today?'*

Ruth: *'Yeah, good. What's for dinner? I'm starving.'*

Mum: *'Chicken.'*

Ruth: *'Do you need a hand?'*

Mum: *'No, you're fine. Much homework?'*

Ruth: *'Yeah, some. I'll make a start before dinner. Hey Mum…you know I was telling you about Rosie? Well, you'll never guess what happened…'*

Tina interacts with her directional daughter with interest and curiosity. She doesn't need to worry about lack of discipline, getting homework completed or trying to stabilise an anxious, overwhelmed teenager. As a directional adolescent, Ruth possesses innate resilience. The adolescent is, for the most part, balanced, disciplined and emotionally regulated. Their dialogue is defined with relative ease and fluency, and there is a quality of mutuality in their relatedness. It looks like Ruth is her favourite, though it's more likely that Tina's experience of parenting is more satisfying with Ruth than with the others. Supervision and support are only minimally required from Tina in relation to parenting this directional adolescent.

Incidentally, teachers do just the same thing. It's halfway through second period and all students should be in their classrooms. The vice-principal Mrs McBride is walking along a quiet corridor and spies a student coming towards her from the far end. It's Kayden. She knows him well as he is frequently sent to her office. Mrs McBride doesn't trust him. She stops, looks serious and asks him in a sharp tone what he is doing out of class. He needed the bathroom. The vice-principal stops and watches Kayden walking down the corridor to ensure that he actually goes back to class. She knows it's likely that he didn't actually need the bathroom at all and has probably been messing about, meandering around for the past fifteen minutes.

Another day it's Zoe making her way along the corridor. Mrs McBride is aware that Zoe struggles with school anxiety and has put several measures in place to support her attendance. Zoe looks unsettled and so she approaches tentatively: *'Are you OK Zoe? Are you feeling anxious? Would you like me to call your mum or would it help to sit with the school nurse for a while?'*

On the day that Mrs McBride meets Ruth, she simply walks by and greets the student warmly. No need to check why she's out of class or where she's going. No need to make sure if she's OK or offer her care. No need to supervise her return to class. The vice-principal trusts this sensible, directional, model student.

The adult world responds to adolescent configuration styles in ways which can sometimes be reinforcing and disconfirming. It's always interesting to me too, not only how parents interact differently with but also how they talk about their teenage children. Depending on the adolescent's developmental location, there is a predictable manner of describing these young people. Let's say Tina bumps into her friend in town, who asks her how the kids are getting on.

Tina's friend:	*'How's Kayden?'* (the impulsive one)
Tina:	(throws her head back and rolls her eyes) *'Aw, he's a wild man altogether. No interest in school at all. There's no talking to him. I don't know what will become of him.'*
Tina's friend:	*'What about Zoe?'* (the inhibitive one)
Tina:	(tilts her head to the side and her tone changes to sympathy) *'Och, the wee pet. She works so hard but she's just so anxious. She's actually getting worse. I just don't know what to do.'*
Tina's friend:	*'And Ruth, how's she getting on?'* (the directional one)
Tina:	(with gratitude and relief in her voice) *'Well thank God Ruth has never given me a minute's bother. She's very good.'*

It interests me how many parents tend not to describe how well the directional adolescent is flourishing in the world but are more likely to express gratitude for what they are *not* doing. This seemingly positive statement usually indicates that there are parenting struggles elsewhere.

Bad Parent Shame

When adolescents are wading through the impulsive and inhibitive stages of development, it is not unusual for parents to blame themselves for the struggles and entrenchment. It is unsurprising to hear them say things such as *'We have four children. The others are great, but we don't know where we've gone wrong with Shane.'* Their bad-parent shame is tangible as they confuse their teenager's developmental twists and turns with being failures as parents. Sometimes parents will even phrase this doubt as an invitation for criticism: *'It's good to get talking to you about Shane. You understand all this and hopefully you'll be able to tell us where we've been going wrong.'* At this point, I usually step in to neutralise the shame in a light-hearted manner by saying something like this:

'Well you know…if this was about being bad parents you would have screwed all four of your kids up. It sounds like the others are doing just fine, so that would suggest this isn't about you being awful parents. My hunch is that Shane isn't responding to your current parenting strategies. We just need some tweaks to find what works. That's all.'

This tends to generate a few smiles and some welcome relief.

The Adolescent with Invisible Needs

For parents, it can be easy to overlook a directional adolescent, particularly when other family members' emotional or behavioural issues are figural, requiring time and attention. The adolescent's empathic adjustment to family life creates more space for others to have their needs met. The directional young person may then play a passive or active part in this dynamic of whose needs take precedence within the family. Family members taking up substantial psychological space may include other siblings or parenting adults.

Nathan shows up passively in his family life. He enjoyed six years as an only child with full parental attention until his brother Aaron was born. Due to a traumatic birth, Aaron required much care and supervision from the outset. At four years of age, Aaron received a diagnosis of ASD. He was a difficult child to soothe and didn't sleep much. Life always has to be on Aaron's terms, and he struggles with rigid coping patterns and a resistance to change or new experiences. Family holidays are a nightmare and Nathan receives regular explanations about why they can't do something or go somewhere – because Aaron doesn't want to or won't be able to tolerate it. The primary consideration at every turn is Aaron's experience. His parents feel a mixture of guilt and gratitude when they think about Nathan. They are so grateful that he is such a good boy and gives them no bother. He just does what he is asked and is so accommodating of Aaron's struggles.

As a child, Nathan played by himself or watched TV when his parents tended to his younger sibling. He artfully learned to suppress his needs and dial down his yearnings for parental attention. Nathan's way of feeling validated and loved has become linked to him not asking for his needs to be met – his parents heap praise on him for being so understanding and patient. On the surface, Nathan appears very resourced and mature – and he is. However, he has creatively adjusted to lifespace conditions by disavowing his needs. The risk is that he will continue to engage in the world in ways which benefit others and validate him for not having needs. As adolescence gets underway, 'just getting on with it' becomes an embedded way of being in the world for Nathan, who finds that self-reliance and not expressing needs is easier for everyone in the family. His parents are also wracked with guilt that their attention and Nathan's life are so defined by

Aaron's needs and that Nathan comes second so much of the time. Parenting is such a dilemma for them, because it feels almost impossible to divide their time equally between their two sons. The demands of parenting a child with entrenched inhibition is overwhelming and all-consuming. They feel so bad about overlooking Nathan and how he misses out on so many potentially enriching family experiences. Their family culture and parenting experience is not what they had anticipated and whilst they love Aaron dearly, they grieve the cost of his rigid presentation for everyone. When they express their guilt at not spending enough time with him or doing enough things together, Nathan takes care of his parents in these moments and assures them that he is fine. He really doesn't mind at all and fully understands. In reality, the adolescent feels that he has to be fine – there is no other option for him. The adolescent describes himself humorously as 'the afterthought', however, unpacking this statement reveals a deep sadness and sense of invisibility. His passive experience of disavowing his needs creates a pseudo-directional presentation.

Similarly, fourteen-year-old Kerry has an older brother and two younger sisters. Her parents separated when she was eleven and the children have remained largely with their mother, Teresa, in the family home, with weekends spent with dad becoming less frequent as time passes. Teresa continues to find it difficult to come to terms with the separation and Kerry sees that mum struggles. The adolescent has become preoccupied with her mother's overwhelm as she witnesses Teresa regularly being upset, constantly on her phone and drinking way too much wine.

Teresa finds it difficult to contain her feelings and increasingly leans on Kerry for support. Mum discloses all manner of inappropriate information to the adolescent who now has adopted a host of new roles within the family. Kerry shifts between being her mother's relationship therapist; co-parent to her siblings; go-between with dad; and homemaker when her mother is unavailable. Kerry also shoulders the burden of the family's financial situation and feels it necessary to find a part-time job so that she can help her mother out.

Teresa expresses gratitude for Kerry being such a great girl and being so helpful. Mum expresses proudly that it is hard to believe her daughter is only fourteen. Kerry is so mature and adult-like and Teresa depends on her much of the time. *What would I do without her?* The teenager has become a parentified adolescent and has assumed a role of adult responsibility. Kerry's prematurely evolved directional configuration style is a creative adjustment to her experience of insufficient support and results in her pushing her feelings and needs to the side in order to help her struggling mother cope. Teresa feels guilty at times about how much she leans on her daughter; however, she needs the support and this dynamic continues. Validation from caretaking and a propensity for disavowing her needs soon became weaved into Kerry's identity. The focus of therapeutic work will be to validate the adolescent's experience and enable her to address hidden yearnings whilst encouraging her mother to identify other sources of support.

Part 3

Therapy

Errata

Chapter 10

Therapy with the Impulsive Adolescent – Working with Parents

Given that encounters with the adult world don't always go well, impulsive teenagers tend not to be enthusiastic about the prospect of going to therapy and it isn't usually their idea to seek it out. These adolescents typically feel that parents, teachers or other professionals involved in their lives are always on their back and commonly the referral is initiated by one or more of these concerned adults. Making the young person's reluctance explicit in a wholly accepting manner at the outset is a useful way to begin to diffuse any intransigence and create the possibility of a meaningful encounter for the adolescent. I usually say something like: *'I don't know too many boys your age who willingly come to therapy, so I'm going to assume that you don't really want to be here.'*

This may appear to be an inconsequential, even counterintuitive remark but it almost always elicits contact. The response is usually a reluctant smile or shrug of the shoulders and we both understand that he can't wait to get the heck out of here.

As the assessment meeting unfolds it will be important to give the adolescent a sense that therapy may offer him a different quality of encounter than he is used to with most adults. My reluctance to join the adult world in mobilising through concern about the adolescent's unacceptable attitude and immature behaviour neutralises shame and generates interest on the part of the teenager. By shifting the focus of dialogue from the adolescent to dynamics within the parent-adolescent field, a little breathing space and hope are created. I am looking out for areas of tension and stuckness, and offering a rationale for ongoing work in a gentle, invitational manner when dilemmas present themselves. During the initial meeting I am attempting to garner a willingness for ongoing involvement from all present.

Simon has type 1 diabetes and is negligent in relation to management of the condition. His parents are very concerned. As well as this, he recently came home from a local disco clearly drunk and has been caught with weed. The teenager is sick and tired of listening to his parents rabbiting on about his irresponsible choices and attitude. He doesn't care about the things that matter to them, such as blood sugars, school and dumb things like keeping his room clean or doing homework. Simon just wishes they would back off and let him get on with his life. He is perfectly happy and considers that it's actually his mum and dad who need to see a therapist

DOI: 10.4324/9781003373599-14

as they are insufferable morons, intent on ruining his life. The last place fifteen-year-old Simon wants to be is sitting in a therapist's office with his parents. Arthur and Donna see the situation quite differently and have sought out the support of a therapist to try to get their son to see sense and start behaving more maturely.

I listen to each person describe their frustration and offer my observation that everyone seems to be stressed out. I share my hunch that Arthur and Donna's approach to parenting their teenage son doesn't appear to be working. In fact, it seems to be serving only to create rupture in their relationship with him. The potential of a different way of engagement for everyone heightens the family's interest and injects relief into the tense and combative relationship between Simon and his parents. They understand now that ongoing work will involve all three.

Therapist:	*'What's it like to feel powerless to influence your son?'*
Donna:	*'It's not good.'*
Therapist:	*'It sounds like you have found yourself parenting in ways which aren't as effective as you might have hoped. I imagine that's frustrating for you.'*
Donna:	*'Definitely.'*
Therapist:	*'What's it like that you have found yourself being the mum who nags?'*
Donna:	*'I hate having to do it. I don't want to be nagging him all the time. You're exactly right, this isn't the type of mother I want to be.'* (Mum softens) *'We used to get on so well. It's so disappointing.'* (She becomes tearful.)
Therapist:	*'You don't sound so much disappointed as heartbroken to me.'*
Donna:	*'I am heartbroken.'*
Therapist:	*'Simon, what's it like to hear your mum and see her tears? It turns out that she doesn't actually want to nag you. Did you know that?'*

Simon shakes his head and looks solemn but interested. This is not a direction he expected the meeting to take and his curiosity is stirring. At this point I let the family know that I would like to try something. I invite dad to swap seats with Simon, assuring the teenager that he doesn't have to do a thing apart from sit in a different chair for a few minutes. Then I ask Arthur to imaginatively become the teenager and speak from his son's experience. I address Arthur as if he is the adolescent:

Therapist	*'So, Simon, these two parents are concerned about you.*
(to Arthur):	*You're not taking yourself very seriously in the world and they just want what's best for you. But what's it like to be their fifteen-year-old son right now?'*
Arthur:	*'It's so annoying. They do my head in with going on and on and on about stupid stuff all the time.'*
Therapist:	*'That sounds tough for you.'*
Arthur:	*'Yeah, they are always telling me what to do.'*

Therapist:	*'What happens to you when your dad is trying to get you to do something or giving you advice?'*
Arthur:	*'I just switch off. I block him out. He's really hard to take.'*
Therapist:	*'You can't stand him in those moments, can you?'*
Arthur:	*'Yeah, I used to love him, but I really can't stand him now.'* (Arthur becomes tearful.)
Therapist:'	*It's hard for you growing up with these parents right now isn't it? They don't seem to get you.'*
Arthur:	*'No, they don't.'*
Therapist:	*'I'm going to guess that it's lonely for you.'*
Arthur:	*'It is. That's why I'm in my room all the time.'*

I invite the pair to swap back again. If the adolescent was more open at this point, I would invite Simon to speak as dad. However, my instinct is that now is not the time. I turn to Arthur and ask him what it was like to become his son. He is saddened at the awareness of what all the nagging and lecturing is doing to the relationship between himself and Simon. It's creating tension and distance between them and Arthur is finding it difficult to reach his son. Without asking anything of Simon, as we do not have sufficient therapeutic contact and there is not enough support for his voice just yet, I offer my reflection:

Therapist:	*'Simon, my hunch is that your dad's guess was pretty accurate?'*
Simon:	*'Yip.'*
Therapist:	*'You're really stressed with all of this, aren't you?'*
Simon:	*'Yip.'*
Therapist:	*'And lonely?'*
Simon shrugs his shoulders nonchalantly.	
Therapist:	*'I'm going to take that shrug of the shoulders as a yes.'*
Simon shrugs his shoulders again, holds my gaze for the first time and nods in agreement.	

I feel a welling up in my chest and a great tenderness in my heart in response to the poignancy of Simon's subtle communication. To be lonely means that he is missing his parents. The power and softness of his yearning infuses the space. I turn to mum and dad:

Therapist:	*'Your son misses you. What's that like to know?'*
Arthur:	*'It's hard.'*
Donna:	*'Yeah, it's hard but it's good too.'*
Therapist:	*'It sounds like you miss him too.'* (Both are tearful now.)
Therapist:	*'Simon, your mum and dad are crying. These are tears of love for you.' Simon doesn't give much away, but I can see that he is moved and more open now.*

After a while, it's time to gather in these pieces of dialogue and offer a way forward.

Therapist: *'So, I'm hearing that all this nagging isn't getting anyone anywhere.*
              It's upsetting for you both as parents. It's frustrating for you Simon.
              And it's not having the intended outcome. It's evident to me that the
              situation between you all as it stands is making everyone miserable.'
              (Everyone nods in agreement.) *'At least we're all clear on one thing*
              then – what's happening between you all isn't working.' (More nod-
              ding.) *'I think I could help with this. Simon, if you're interested in*
              coming back, then one of the things I would like to do is to get your
              parents to stop nagging you. How would that be?'
Simon: *'I'd be fucking delighted.'*
Therapist: *'Well to be fair, I think your parents would also be fucking delighted.'*

Everyone laughs and there is a lighthearted moment of joining.

Parent Strategy Work

Meeting alone with parents is a useful next step. The initial stage of this work is
to support them to develop an understanding of why their teenage child is presenting so 'unreasonably'. As they hear an explanation of limbic activation, Arthur
and Donna begin to appreciate that their son's behaviour is a matter of course and
totally normal for his stage of development. Being governed by the desire to feel
good and belong with peers, and at the same time not having much access to thinking and self-reflection, future-orientation or empathy offers a welcome explanation to these parents. Giving space to Arthur and Donna to talk more deeply about
Simon's presentation helps them feel more held and understood. Shifting the focus
to their current parenting style and explaining to them that the three very typical
ways of reacting to impulsive teens are nagging, lecturing and punishing supports
them to reflect on and dialogue about their responses. They see the redundancy of
these approaches and recognise the need for a new way forward, which not only
involves support for Simon, but also requires revising their approach to parenting.
The tone of urgency and frustration which infused their initial contact with me has
morphed into interest and relief. They are grateful that someone understands and
seems to know what they are doing.

The next stage is to evolve their parenting into a better developmental fit.
I explain that the goal of this new approach is the encouragement of frontal lobe
activation. Their son's strong limbic energy means that he lacks discipline and any
real inclination or capacity to contain his impulses. Nagging him to tone down his
dopamine flow, lecturing him about how he ought to be conducting himself and
punishing him for being developmentally on point will not do the trick. These will
only serve to reinforce limbic activity. We are coming towards the end of our first
parental strategy meeting and I invite both parents to continue to reflect on what we
have talked about today and to notice how they relate to their son – not changing
anything just yet, but just noticing.

During the following meeting Arthur and Donna report how much they rely on nagging, lecturing and punishment as their principal modes of contact with Simon when his choices are met with their disapproval. Crucially, the parents have started to notice how their son responds in these moments. Arthur and Donna admit that up until now they had put his inclination to disengage with his parents down to teen-age hormones. They are seeing it differently now – appreciating that their contact with Simon may have been antagonistic and disconfirming at times. This break-through moment is an important dimension of change. New strategies are difficult for parents to commit to unless they come to appreciate the redundancy of their existing approach.

The next step for Arthur and Donna is to implement some bite-your-lip parent-ing responses, which is a middle ground between the old and the new. At moments when they would typically have relied on some lecturing or reprimanding, I sug-gest they let this pass and instead choose to reflect on what they might do dif-ferently. For example, ignored requests to help around the house or to complete homework would previously have resulted in these parents giving out and making comments about Simon's lack of respect and irresponsible mindset. These remarks would be met with the inevitable and predictable eye-rolling and attitude. Further response from parents often resulted in an all-out battle ending with the adolescent muttering something about his parents being assholes and some door slamming. Interactions such as these do two things: the teenager becomes even less willing to undertake the requested task than before, or does so with a huffy strop, and there is now a little more tension and dislocation between him and his parents. In addition, the emotional hangover from their exchange sets up the next interaction, perpetu-ating the shame cycle for everyone. I suggest to the parents that they stop trying to improve their son's attitude, choices and behaviours by pointing out what he needs to do and where he is going wrong. This is antagonistic contact.

The next part of the experiment is to meet him with an open heart. Arthur and Donna are tasked with taking space to reflect on their feelings of love towards their son prior to interacting with him. I name that their intention is to relate to Simon from this place of love and deep acceptance. Additionally, when they are interacting with their son, I suggest to the parents to refrain from asking questions. Impulsively configured adolescents tend to be withholding in their dialogue with adults, and so, parents tend to fall into a bind of interrogative contact: *How is school going? Do you have any homework? What time do you call this? Are you still playing that Xbox? Have you loaded the dishwasher yet?* This tends to close adolescents down even more, whereas these parents are attempting to create more richness in their relating.

Repairing Relationship

Arthur describes feeling less and less close to his son. Their shared interest in Gaelic football was an important way to bond through Simon's childhood. Father and son went to matches together and Arthur coached the under-ten team when

Simon played for the club. Simon also played the fiddle and Arthur, who loves traditional Irish music and plays flute, took him to lessons and competitions. They sometimes played together, which delighted them both. However, during the teenage years, Simon's interest wanes, and he gives up football and music. Arthur tries to get him interested in both activities again, without success. All his son seems to want to do now is spend time in his room on screens or hanging out with his friends. His relationship with the adolescent is infused with disappointment, concern and frustration. As we unpack this, Arthur begins to see that these feelings are shaping contact with his son. He is ready to try something different.

On his drive home from work each day, Arthur contemplates his relationship with Simon. He recalls Donna telling him that she was pregnant and how excited he felt. He remembers the first time he held Simon and how he thought his heart was going to burst with love. He calls to mind significant moments through the years and finds that when he does this, he softens and feels tenderly about his son. He reminds himself that his son is growing and developing, and there were tricky times in the past – when Simon was teething or having tantrums as a toddler. The patience and holding he demonstrated as a dad way back then is required in just the same measure today. He understands more now about why his son presents the way he does, and he feels more compassion. When he arrives home, his intention is to support Simon to feel loved by him. He goes to his son's bedroom and knocks on the door.

Arthur: 'Hi Simon, it's good to see you.'
Simon: 'What?'
Arthur: 'I hope your day was good. I imagine you're glad school's over.'
Simon: 'I'm playing a game with my friends.' (Sighs and looks impatient.)
Arthur: 'Would you like me to get you a drink or anything?'
Simon: 'No, I'm OK.'
Arthur: 'OK, well if you want anything just let me know. I'll let you get back to your game.'

This interaction is difficult for Arthur who has to bite his lip considerably. He wants to tell his son to get off the game console, to get his homework done, tidy his room and remove the mould-covered plates and cups, to open the window and let some fresh air in and to have some manners and talk more respectfully to his father. He also wants to ask him what he's eaten today, if he's checked his blood sugars recently and see if he needs insulin. Arthur does not trust Simon to responsibly attend to his diabetes management. However, he knows where these conversation threads will lead. We will get to all these things but healing their relationships and neutralising the shame that has crept in is the primary focus for now. Arthur is trying to step into a less combative and more actively supportive role. Over time, these short exchanges, whilst challenging for him, will have created welcome relief for Simon who now doesn't always feel that his dad is on his back. The adolescent steadily becomes less defensive as he begins to trust that his parents are less willing to shame him.

It's difficult for parents to step back momentarily from expressing their concern and keeping on the back of their adolescent, however, if they can be supported to see that their intuitive parenting approach is not actually very effective, they tend to be more willing to experiment. Limbic energy is not subdued by shaming someone, but by encouraging greater sophistication in functioning – that is to say, by bringing the frontal lobes online. Parenting strategies are aimed at teaching adolescents to contain their impulses by promoting the development of future-orientation, thinking and empathy.

Transactional Parenting

Next, I help the parents draw up two lists – things that are important to them and things that are important to Simon. Impulsive teens like to feel good, so there are usually plenty items to put on the list: time with friends, youth club, discos, money, clothes, electronics, concert tickets, driving lessons, trips, acrylic nails, cosmetics, beauty and hair appointments to name a few. In today's world, parenting takes place within a culture of indulgence. In many households, young people are gifted these things freely and parents are constantly treating their teenage children. For example, Simon shows his mum a picture of a cool pair of expensive trainers which he wants. Donna pops them in the online shopping cart, and they arrive a few days later. Meanwhile, she can't get him to take the dirty dishes from his bedroom to the kitchen. She then experiences frustration and looks for empathy from her son, both of which are simply going to irritate him.

'You still haven't tidied your room? I spent over a hundred and fifty pounds on those trainers the other day and I don't get as much as a thank you. I'm out working to give you a decent life and this is the response I get from you. The least you could do is take those dishes downstairs like I told you. All I'm asking for is that you pull your weight in this house.'

Donna is hoping that her words might have this kind of an effect:

Wow my mum really is so giving and selfless, spending all of that money on a pair of trainers I don't actually need, but just want. Demonstrating my gratitude by complying with her request to tidy my room is not much to ask. I'll just pause this online game with my friends which I'm winning, to gather up the dirty dishes, go downstairs and load the dishwasher.

The parents' list includes behaviours they wish their teenager would do more of or do less of, for example, household chores, homework, diabetes management, sleep and wake times, drinking, swearing, managing health issues. Not on the list are the adolescent's attitude or level of respect for parents. The focus is on concrete, tangible, practical issues. In truth, most parents want very little, including Donna and Arthur. They would like Simon to do a bit of homework, keep his room reasonably tidy and be more careful with his diabetes management. That's it.

Transactional parenting is the trading off of dopamine generators with frontal lobe-activating behaviours. As the parents move into this new mode of contact, they select one item from each list. As a starting point, it's important to choose something relatively straightforward and realistic. Three hours of study every night for someone who doesn't spend any time on homework in return for being able to spend Saturday afternoon in town with friends is not going to succeed. The ask is too big and the reward is not worth it. Donna and Arthur feel that the diabetes management is of most concern and urgency, so they select this. It is Simon's birthday in six weeks, and he has asked for a pair of the highest quality, highest priced ear buds. The intensity of the challenge should be matched by the strength of his investment in how he will benefit from the transaction. It turns out that Simon would like a new pair of ear buds – and this potential transaction looks like a good coupling. Their prior parenting strategy would have been to threaten not to get the ear buds but give them to their son anyway…whilst nagging constantly about his blood sugars, insulin and diet. Now they will approach the situation a little differently…starting with an apology. The parents ask Simon to come into the sitting room later that evening.

Donna: 'We want to talk to you about something son.'
Simon looks uneasy and is braced for a reprimand about something or other.
Arthur: 'We've been doing a lot of reflecting about us as parents and we've noticed how much we go on about your diabetes. We'd like to apologise to you because the nagging must be never-ending for you.'
Donna: 'Yeah, we would like to stop doing that. How does that sound to you?'
Simon: 'Finally!'
Arthur: 'So, here's the deal – let's see if you're interested. We're going to get you those ear buds that you want for your birthday. We'd rather not and they're very expensive, but we're willing to get you them because they're the ones you want.'
Simon: 'Happy days.'
Donna: 'There's one condition: every day from tomorrow until your birthday your blood sugars don't go over 14. That means you have to check your blood sugars and give yourself insulin at mealtimes. We're always getting notifications during the day that your blood sugars are sky high and that's stressful for us and stressful for you.'
Arthur: 'We don't want to have to interfere as we know it bothers you…but because you don't check blood sugar levels and take insulin, we keep having to step in to get you regulated.'
Donna: 'And it would be great not to be getting notifications every day.'
Arthur: 'So, this way we could trust you to take care of your diabetes, we'd back off AND you'd get your ear buds. How does this sound to you?'
Simon: 'Yeah, good.'
Donna: 'Would you be willing to make it a deal then?'
Simon: 'Yeah.'
Arthur: 'Now it means that if you go above 14 – even one day – the deal is off. Are you OK with that?'
Simon: 'Yeah.'

This almost sounds too good to be true...because it probably is. One of the learning points for the adolescent is the development of discipline and consistency. This doesn't happen overnight, so parents must anticipate failure. Impulsive people are full of good intentions and Simon is one hundred per cent resolved to keep his side of the deal. He couldn't be more sincere about his pledge to keep his diabetes in check. Mind you...have you ever set out on a diet and not stuck to it? Have you ever sworn off alcohol or chocolate and fallen at the first hurdle? Alas, there is quite a discrepancy between experiencing an impulse and containing it. So, not if, but *when* Simon fails and his blood sugars skyrocket, his parents introduce the second part of their strategy. Instead of coming in with the nagging about the need for their son to take his medical condition seriously and the implications if he doesn't, they appeal to his need for dopamine.

Arthur: *'You didn't keep your end of the bargain so we're not keeping ours. No ear buds for your birthday. That was the deal.'*
Simon: *'But that's not fair. It wasn't even my fault. You see I was with the boys and we were playing football at break time and it was raining so we had to use the side door and my bag was in my form class and I...'*
Arthur: *'OK, new deal...the ear buds are back on the table and you'll get them exactly one week after your birthday if you want to try again. How's that?'*
Simon: *'OK.'*
Arthur: *'And if you go above 14 again, we push it back for another week. You'll get your ear buds, but it depends on YOU when you get them.'*

During the first failure episode, Simon is annoyed at his parents for disappointing him but as he sticks with it, despite stumbling, he projects less on to them and becomes more aware that the reason he's not getting his ear buds is because of his lack of willingness to manage his diabetes. The penny starts to drop. Parental consistency and patience are key for this new transactional mode of parenting to succeed. Unrealistic expectations, frustration and reverting to the previously ineffective strategies only aggravate the situation.

It is also important for parents not to change the parameters of the deal in reaction to something else. For example, when Simon thumps his younger brother for being annoying and really hurts him, it's very tempting to threaten him with not getting the ear buds now at all. However, this is unfair and confusing for the adolescent. There will be other opportunities to hold him to account for his wrongdoing, such as the disco next Friday night. He will not be permitted to attend now, but no deal will have been broken in the process. The only factor taken into consideration in relation to getting the ear buds should be Simon's diabetes management. Once one transaction is going relatively smoothly, I support the parents to introduce additional ones, though I caution Donna and Arthur not to bamboozle the teenager with too many at a time.

Parental involvement in the work with impulsive adolescents is so important in order to support attunement and neutralise any shame which may have emerged as a result of fixed, ineffective patterns of relating. New strategies empower parents and also go a long way to supporting the adolescent's developmental journey. Stress levels all round are diminished.

Antagonistic Parenting Approaches

In this example, Simon's parents, Arthur and Donna, are themselves directional adults. They each have a well-developed sense of self and a capacity to reflect both on their relationship with their son and on their parenting approach. Unfortunately, not every parent demonstrates this level of functioning. This creates limitations to parental intervention work. The art of parenting impulsive adolescents requires empathic resonance, developmental attunement and patience in abundance. Sadly, not all parents are organised in this way. People who remain entrenched in an impulsive or inhibitive configuration style beyond adolescence and who then become parents themselves tend to struggle when rearing an impulsive adolescent. Involving these parents in the therapeutic process results in varying degrees of success.

The Impulsive Parent

Fourteen-year-old Leo's parents separated a number of years ago and he lives between both homes during the week. He is a typically impulsive teen for his age – more interested in gaming than homework, not inclined to do housework, not feeling tired at night but not being able to get up for school in the morning, and so on. It is discovered that Leo has been self-harming and so he is referred for psychotherapy. Working through the aftermath of his parents' separation is the predominant theme in our sessions and, with an eye to developmental process, we also address Leo's impulsivity and the corresponding parenting approach. The adolescent's mother, Iris, gets it – she is able to understand her son from this new perspective. Slower now to judge his behaviours, mum has let go of her expectations for him to magically become directional. Iris also has the capacity to appraise her own parenting style. She realises how her intuitive nagging, lecturing, threatening and punishing neither elicits the desired response nor enhances the relationship with her son in any way. In fact, she sees now that it does the opposite. Iris approaches this new strategy purposefully and with equanimity – and it gradually works. Day-to-day life is transformed in their home and stress levels diminish considerably.

Leo's dad, Richard, on the other hand, understands the concept and has the *intention* of approaching the situation with his son in this new manner. However, he lacks the attributes required to patiently and consistently apply this transactional approach. Richard was an impulsive adolescent himself – an experimenter and risk taker, tempestuous and quite a handful for his own parents and teachers to manage. This configuration style has never fully abated and whilst he lives relatively successfully as an adult, Richard continues to struggle with impulsive traits such as emotional reactivity and a penchant for gambling, drinking and overspending. His intuitive parenting skills emerge from the limbic system and are a feeling response to his son's attitudes and behaviours. There are occasional times when he manages to interrupt his impulse and access a more considered response, but for the most part Richard reacts spontaneously.

For example, Leo is spending a few nights at his dad's house and has a soccer match on Saturday morning. As impulsive teens are prone to poor forward planning and foresight, he has left his football boots at mum's. Richard, who when picking Leo up asked him if he had everything he needed, is immediately irritated and gives out to the adolescent. *'How could you not think?'* When his son closes down, this infuriates Richard and he is now off-balance. He shames Leo by dragging up past behaviour – *'you're always…you never…you need to…'* and in his emotionally dysregulated state dad now starts to bad-mouth his ex-wife *'she lets you away with far too much'*. Richard's failure to pause, see the bigger picture and develop an attuned response to the situation results in unconstrained and inappropriate shaming and dumping. Afterwards dad feels a hint of remorse, but quickly assumes the defended position of placing the responsibility for his outburst firmly with his son. If Leo wasn't so forgetful and so worried about checking his phone, he would have remembered the boots and dad wouldn't have had to lose his temper. This whole episode, including Richard becoming off-balance, was his son's fault.

Richard announces that the teenager will not be going to football in the morning or any other morning until he develops a better attitude. Leo messages his mum to tell her what has happened and his mum steps in to mop up the situation. Dad's position is in conflict with an important negotiation which has been unfolding between Leo and his parents: if he studies for one hour each evening after school, he gets to his football training twice during the week and to his match on a Saturday. So far, the adolescent is keeping his end of the deal fairly well, but dad is threatening to derail the whole transaction. Iris calls her ex-husband to remind him how important it is to demonstrate consistency as parents with this new transactional approach. Mum points out how well their son is responding to this deal so far. She supports dad to find balance once more. Iris also soothes an upset and angry son and drives over with the boots. The football game and the transactional parenting are back on. An impulsive parent's contact tends to be reactive and inflammatory, punctuated by shouting matches, moodiness, huffing and blaming. It can be difficult for Richard to remain consistent and measured in his responses and he requires much more support from me than Iris.

The Inhibitive Parent

Seventeen-year-old Katie has always been an impulsive person. She is unmotivated in general and tends to overindulge on nights out with her friends. Her mother, Annmarie, has an inhibitive mindset, thinking rather than feeling her way through life and focused on an externalised sense of self and family. Katie's attitude and behaviour are at odds with her mother's expectations about how she ought to be conducting herself. The adolescent's impulsivity has created plenty of stress and chaos for her and her parents over the years with lower grades than she is capable of, school reports which make for interesting reading, escapades with friends which have backfired and a recent abortion following unprotected sex. Her parents have had enough.

As we commence the shift to transactional parenting, they have all agreed to trade off driving lessons for study hours: if Katie completes six hours of study per week for her upcoming exams, she will have a Saturday morning driving lesson. This seems like a tall order, though the adolescent is motivated as these driving lessons are important to her. Katie is hoping to share her older sister's car as soon as she gets her licence. The adolescent also wants to do well in her exams in order to get to university, so there is a fairly strong degree of investment in the transaction. She is doing her best with the studying, but it's hit and miss, some weeks being better than others. One-to-one therapy with the adolescent is supporting her to adopt greater discipline and responsibility. Katie was doing zero study prior to this, so she is moving in the right direction, even if she does not always hit the target.

Annmarie struggles to make the transition to transactional parenting, often losing sight of the bigger picture of what we are trying to achieve and reverting to nagging and lecturing as a reflexive response to the recklessness of her daughter's behaviour. When Katie breaks her end of the bargain, rather than focusing on reworking the deal for the following week, trusting that her daughter will feel the sting of missing out on a driving lesson, Annmarie mobilises through fear and urgency. In order to manage her anxiety and discomfort, mum reminds Katie how important her studies are, what an intelligent girl she is and how Katie has the world at her feet if only she would apply herself. When this doesn't elicit the required response, Annmarie attempts to get through to her daughter by adopting a more antagonistic approach. Mum compares the adolescent to her academically successful older sister and cousins, telling her that she's letting the family down. She criticises Katie's friends, makes snide remarks about her weight and searches her bedroom, finding and reading her diary. Dad, who is on board and progressing well with the new transactional strategy work, is pressured by Annmarie to involve himself in giving out to the adolescent and lambasted when he is reluctant to do so.

Annmarie is at her wit's end at the possibility that Katie might fail her exams. She is coming from a place of care and concern and has her daughter's best interests at heart – albeit from a one-dimensional inhibitive perspective of external validation. Mum is doing the best she can but cannot help herself with pushing relentlessly in order to get Katie to study. She does not see that her approach is having a detrimental effect on both the issue of Katie's grades and on the relationship with her daughter itself. The transaction which started out with promise has morphed back into persistent niggling and pressure.

Consequently, Katie experiences her mother as controlling and shaming, feeling that Annmarie tries to manage every facet of her life. The adolescent feels belittled and reduced to an extension of her mother's self-image – if Katie was more like her sister, had better friends, was thinner and more studious then she would be more loveable and more acceptable. This inhibitive mother's contact with her daughter not only alienates the adolescent but also damages Katie's self-perception. Parenting strategy work with Annmarie has minimal impact given her entrenchment as an inhibitive parent.

Chapter 11

Therapy with the Impulsive Adolescent – One-to-one Work

Individual work with the impulsive adolescent complements parental strategy work, so that everyone is moving in the same direction with a similar focus, that is to say, frontal lobe activation. Simply engaging in verbal dialogue with a fifteen-year-old will not do the trick. As well as the risk of boring the adolescent to death, I can be sure that the young person will struggle to integrate the meaning of the conversation and the words will be lost on them. A primary intervention with adolescents is understanding the self, and it helps to physically *see* a representation of the lifespace rather than simply attempting to abstractly conceive of it through verbal constructs.

When we meet together for the first time, I begin by offering my hunch to Simon that he very likely regrets saying that he'd attend another session. This statement is met by a smile and we have a fleeting moment of joining which he hadn't bargained on. Respectful irreverence used sparingly and in a timely manner can decompress a tense therapeutic moment. Opting out of power struggles is always a winner with impulsive adolescents. It grounds the therapeutic space more deeply to name what's going on, which in Simon's case is that he doesn't really want to be here. It is preferable to setting about convincing him to stay or engaging with him as if he's a fully compliant client. It bodes well to remember that one never wins a power struggle with an impulsive teen.

Knowing what not to do is important with impulsive adolescents. They often don't see the need to be in therapy and don't share adult-world concerns about their life, so a focus on this is met with indifference. The therapeutic equivalent of parental advice-giving and lecturing is psychoeducation, but impulsive adolescents tend to learn from experience – from the inside out – so this may well not work. These kids don't see the bigger picture of their lives and tend not to have language for their emotional experience, so asking them to self-reflect is usually a road to nowhere. Asking them to start a therapeutic conversation can be difficult and the therapist will usually be met with a blank stare and shrug of the shoulders. It's a challenge to support a non-reflective, noncompliant, immature adolescent who is creating concern for the well-meaning adults in his life. That is, unless you find ways to get him interested in himself so that you can reach him and initiate frontal lobe energy. Making his life visual, tangible and three-dimensional – so that he

DOI: 10.4324/9781003373599-15

Figure 11.1 Simon's Lifespace

is given a new vantage point from which to view himself and his lifespace – is a powerful and intriguing mode of doing just this. *Sandspace* (a mode of working developmentally with adolescents using sand and figures I have created) as an adjunct to and visual extension of the dialogue, goes a long way to supporting the meaning-making process.

I invite Simon to sit back and hear my take on things…actually not just to hear but to *see* my take on things. I visually sculpt an aspect of his lifespace in the sand (Figure 11.1).

Therapist: *'I want to try to understand your life, particularly what's happening with your parents. I'd like to help as it seems stressful for you. So, here's my thoughts.'* (I describe Simon's life from my empathic viewpoint whilst making a visual representation of what I'm saying, starting with validating his impulses.) *'Let's put you centre stage. You like to hang out and game with your friends. It's been discovered that you drink, and smoke weed. You're not much interested in schoolwork and you don't care about having diabetes. Right?'* (Left cluster Figure 11.1)

Simon: *'Right.'*

Therapist: *'There are pros and cons to having these impulses. You have a lot of fun with your friends or getting drunk or high. It's much more* enjoyable to spend your evening gaming than studying. And not having the bother of checking your blood sugars. Right?'

Simon: 'Yeah.'

Therapist: 'But the downside is that people are on your back about these things. That stresses you out and you get upset. And then you get angry and that gets you into more trouble. School isn't going especially well, given that you have no interest in studying and it looks like you're heading for failure for these next round of exams. And because of the alcohol and weed and eating what you want and not checking your blood sugars, your parents don't trust you, so you're treated like a kid. Right?' (Centre cluster Figure 11.1)

Simon: 'Yip.'

Therapist: 'And my guess is that you don't want to be treated like a kid anymore. You want to be given responsibility for your own life and your own decisions, without other people interfering. And you want your freedom.'

Simon: 'Yeah.'

Therapist: 'OK, here's the thing…they come as a set of three, not two: the package is freedom, responsibility and trust. That's just how the universe works. If you want freedom and responsibility for your life, you have to trade those off with trust. And, to be fair, it sounds like your track record on trust may not be just spectacular.'

Simon: 'Fair enough.'

Therapist: 'So, you don't have much or any concern about how you're living your life?'

Simon: 'Nope.'

Therapist: 'OK, I get that…but here's the thing. Someone has to hold the concern about your life and if it's not going to be you, it's going to be the adult world. For you, that's mostly your parents and teachers.' (Right cluster Figure 11.1) 'It basically works like this…until you show some signs of concern and give them some reasons to trust you, they'll be hovering over your life managing your freedom and taking responsibility. And that's going to continue to stress you. I mean…you're fifteen. I'm not sure what your plans are, but let's say you want to head to college, that means you have another three years living at home with your parents in charge of your life and not trusting you. How would that be?'

Simon: 'Not good.'

Therapist: 'What would you like to do anyway actually?'

Simon: 'I either want to be a doctor or work with cars or be a horse trainer.'

Therapist: 'All of those sound interesting. I like your options and I'd love to hear about them all some time. But right now, let's focus on getting your parents off your back and getting you more freedom in your life. OK?'

Simon:	'OK.'
Therapist:	'How are we doing anyway – you and me?'
Simon:	'Yeah, good.'
Therapist:	'So, basically you want to start giving them reasons to trust you. You need to be smart about this Simon. I imagine it feels like your parents have all the power and influence over your life…but that's not it. You actually have the power – if you're willing to experiment. Do you want to hear my plan?'
Simon:	'Sure.' (The adolescent puts his hood up and I sense ambivalence.)
Therapist:	'When I spoke with your parents, they mentioned something about you not checking your blood sugars very well and they keep having to step in. So, they have zero trust in you around your diabetes – would that be a fair comment?'
Simon:	'Yeah.'
Therapist:	'I hear there are a pair of ear buds at stake. How's that going anyway?'
Simon:	'Not good.'
Therapist:	'Let's look at the bigger picture…it seems that you'll get so much more than just a fancy pair of ear buds if you sort out the diabetes. Hear me out: you start checking your blood sugars every time before you eat and take insulin if you need it. Your mum and dad no longer get notifications which stress them out. They're impressed with you. They start trusting you. At the minute, because you don't look after your diabetes, they're reluctant to let you go places. So, all of a sudden, you start getting more freedom because they trust you to be concerned about your diabetes. And there's no more nagging about diabetes – it's a conversation that just doesn't happen anymore. AND I know from talking to other people your age who have diabetes that it's really oppressive. It never goes away and when your blood sugars are unstable it affects your mood and lots of stuff. What would it be like to have diabetes become a much smaller part of your life?'
Simon:	'Yeah good. When I walk into a room, they just ask "what are your blood sugars like?" I'm like, "hello, I'm fucking here too".'
Therapist:	'They see your blood sugars before they see you?'
Simon:	'Yeah. It's really fucking annoying.' (The hood comes down again as he is activated.)
Therapist:	'I imagine that's a lonely feeling.'
Simon:	'They care more about my blood sugars than they do about me.'
Therapist:	'I feel sad imagining how invisible you might feel sometimes. And you know, that's a good example of them holding the concern for you. They don't trust that you've checked your blood sugars or that they're at all regulated. So, your mum and dad feel the need to step in and hold the concern.'
Simon:	'I guess.'

Therapist:	'Now if you start checking those blood sugars…you know what will happen…they'll start seeing you more. You'll walk into a room and they'll say, "hello Simon, how are you?" not "how are your blood sugars?"…because they'll trust you.'
Simon:	'Maybe.'
Therapist:	'It's going to be really annoying having to check up on your diabetes, but it sounds like the payoff might be worth it for you? And of course, if you don't want to do it you absolutely don't have to. Mind you, you know the alternative…they'll continue to step in with concern. That's just how this is going to work unfortunately. Your parents care about you and they seem to be unwilling to let your health go unchecked.'
Simon:	'That makes sense.'
Therapist:	'Are you willing to keep experimenting with it?'
Simon:	'Yeah, I suppose.'
Therapist:	'And don't worry if it doesn't work out. There's more to life than ear buds. I'm sure you have a perfectly good set of headphones – or your parents might be open to getting you a less expensive brand.'

These cheap alternatives do not interest Simon, though he now grasps that the ball is decidedly in his court with regards to him getting the ear buds that he wants. With the aid of *Sandspace*, the adolescent is visually figuring out that certain decisions he makes will have anticipated outcomes. He begins to think in a more reality-based manner, considers the future implications of his behaviours and sees the predictable adult-world responses. The construction of his experience in the *Sandspace* offers Simon choice points. Simon lacks discipline and a sense of personal responsibility in his life, and this new perspective clearly demonstrates to him the implications of uncontained impulses. The adolescent embodies his frontal lobe, so to speak, and from a new vantage point, sees the consequences of his limbic lifespace played out before his eyes. Deeper self-reflection has been initiated. The dilemma of him being such an impulsive adolescent, which was being held by his parents, has now been tactfully placed at Simon's feet. New perspectives, presented visually and three-dimensionally through *Sandspace* work, support this awareness.

To be sure, this intervention alone will not be sufficient to contain his impulses and fast-track Simon to becoming a directional adolescent…but it is an important start. I, much like parents, also have to expect failure. Therapeutic work is helped along with the reflective opportunities offered by the inevitable chaos and trouble which punctuates an impulsive adolescent's life: failed exams, drunken nights sometimes ending in A&E due to his medical condition and showdowns with parents to name a few. Simon is not going to transform his choices overnight – what this intervention will have done is supported him to see the meaning and motivation of his behaviours. He knows now that he can't have it both ways – if he doesn't step up to the mark, adults will step in with concern in an attempt to manage the situation. His parents will stress him out – not because they are insufferable idiots, as he previously thought, but because they are picking up the slack where he is falling short.

Sandspace kickstarts the self-reflective capacity and bigger-picture thinking supporting adolescents to discern and appraise predictable outcomes of present and future choices. Impulsive adolescents gradually learn the art of discipline – consistently making decisions based on what's the best way forward rather on what they feel like doing. *Sandspace* will be an ongoing extension of dialogue to support understanding and choicefulness. With this particular client, other therapeutic themes include his relationship to diabetes and its impact on his developing sense of self.

The Challenge of Entrenched Impulsivity

When adolescents are entrenched in limbic activity, it can be much more challenging to influence them developmentally. Everything is exaggerated: their choices are more outrageous, their moods are more intense, their reactions are more amped up and their self-concern is negligible. Shay, aged seventeen, becomes bored, frustrated and irritable very quickly. Emotional regulation is not part of his repertoire of skills. Shay's impulsivity has become more pronounced during the adolescent years. He uses drugs and alcohol, has attached himself to a peer group of much older teens and engages in plenty of other risky activity disapproved of by parents. He rarely attends his training course, has a short attention span, loses everything, gets into debt, is noncompliant and has aggressive outbursts. The adolescent is always in trouble and the adults in his world find it difficult to reach and influence him. Throughout childhood they tried rewarding positive behaviour with all manner of stars, stickers and treats to no avail. Time-out, loss of privileges and being grounded were also implemented without success. Any form of discipline now goes unheeded by the adolescent as family members dread the aftermath of each weekend's antics and his volatile moods.

After crashing his mother's car which he drove without permission, licence or insurance whilst drunk, Shay finally and sheepishly agrees to go to therapy. I explain to his mother that in order for the work to be effective, the pace and timing will need to accommodate her son's impulsive rhythm. Before too long the adolescent's remorseful posture wanes and his disinterest becomes figural. Expecting his attendance at weekly therapy sessions is not feasible. Instead, scheduling therapy when he is in a state of regret following an inevitable screw-up or debacle will usually ensure two things: greater willingness to show up and a much less defended posture. Parent strategy work continues as I support mum to create appropriate boundaries where she can and to adopt a non-inflammatory contact style with Shay. In relation to one-to-one work with the adolescent, I suggest we leave the therapy for now, letting him know that he is welcome back if he so wishes. Shay is sure he won't cross the threshold of my office again. My hunch is that I may see him within the next couple of months.

Shay's drinking and drug use land him back in therapy with me within the predicted time frame. He is filled with regret and with good intentions to abandon his impulsive lifestyle. This remorseful stage translates as a momentary sojourn into his still developing and not fully interconnected cerebral cortex where he drums up unrealistic, half-baked plans which fade from memory once the dopamine crave hits again: akin to the alcoholic swearing off drink following a binge. Nonetheless, this short-lived episode presents a window of opportunity to create more understanding and presentation of choice points for the adolescent, even though the behaviours will continue for now. I use the *Sandspace* to create dilemmas about how failure to take himself seriously and uncontained limbic energy are drawing concern from adults – not just a frustrated mother or teacher.

The extent of his impulsivity is matched by the level of adult-world involvement: he is known to police and may have a criminal record if upcoming court proceedings do not rule in his favour. Shay expresses his fear and anxiety with regards to the fallout of his impulsive lifestyle at times. Other times he doesn't care. We schedule another appointment which he attends only to get his mother off his back, but this time he is fully limbic-activated and back in the dopamine cycle. He isn't bothered now about the implications of his behaviour, is unwilling to take ownership of his reactions and tells me that he outbursts at his mother *'because she does his fuckin' head in'*. He is defended against his own integrity and it is much harder to reach him this time. Sculpting this more indifferent experience, without judgement, in the *Sandspace* where Shay is dissociated from concern and responsibility, will hardly stimulate notable transformation just now. However, these lifespace representations stay with clients long after the session is over, and our visual dialogue will plant seeds for him to accept the hollowness of his denial. There will be more chaos, more regret and more flashes of self-reflection. Each one will present an opportunity for greater awareness and ownership. Therapy proceeds at a snail's pace.

Working with a strongly impulsive young person solely at an individual level can feel like a never-ending process of two steps forward and ten steps back as they struggle with intense limbic activity. Prosocial ventures, as an adjunct to therapy, are a wonderful way to stir the frontal lobes into action – substituting the buzz of a quick dopamine hit with personally rewarding and socially meaningful enterprise. I liaise with Shay's mother and keyworker to organise his participation in a project where old bicycles are refurbished and made available to the community. This project affords the adolescent an experience of feeling good which also generates empathy, social awareness and great personal satisfaction. The novelty of getting plenty of dopamine *and* generating a positive feedback loop is compelling. The creation of a space where Shay is more than the sum of his impulses and their fallout is validating and inspiring for him, although he continues to struggle with his impulsive reflex.

The challenge when attempting to support an adolescent who endures entrenched impulsivity is to keep them sufficiently interested in attending therapy in the first place. It is a hopeful sign when they keep showing up and it is important not to give up on young people who are difficult to reach. I have a client who was deeply and brutally traumatised as a child and who, as a result, configured as a very impulsive adolescent. He first came to me when he was fifteen and is now thirty-two years old. We are getting there.

Chapter 12

Therapy with the Inhibitive Adolescent – Working with Parents

Inhibitive adolescents are attempting to function in the world whilst plagued with psychological, emotional and interpersonal insecurity. This manifests as a deep conviction that they are inadequate and unacceptable, as well as a pervasive sense of discomfort in the world. As anxiety and restriction dominate their teenage child's experience, parents feel limited in their capacity to influence and reverse this lifespace formation which becomes increasingly entrenched.

Margaret and Bernard are terribly worried about their daughter Colleen and have sought therapeutic support for her. Inside the fifteen-year old's comfort zone is her mother, a friendship group of which she is on the periphery, her bedroom, her drama class, certain foods and her screens. Colleen feels pressured by the social and academic aspects of school attendance. The adolescent also experiences interacting with people with whom she is unfamiliar or being in groups as threatening. She is constantly flooded with negative thoughts. Anxiety symptoms include panic attacks and OCD. Family life has been hijacked as parents and siblings have had to accommodate Colleen's anxiety. School mornings are stressful for everyone. Colleen's panic and stalling means she is inevitably late, and Margaret has consequently had to adjust her working hours, allowing for the adolescent's time-consuming morning routine.

I meet the adolescent and her parents online for the contact assessment as Colleen tends to feel overwhelmed entering unfamiliar spaces. The adolescent sits quietly and passively next to her mother as parents begin describing with urgency their daughter's anxiety symptoms. I describe the anxious lifespace and speak generically about its configuration: the comfort zone, all that is threatening to it and anxiety symptoms at its edge. This resonates with everyone and supports a deepening of the dialogue. I note to them that the underlying issue is likely to be that the adolescent lacks faith in herself and that this is what needs to be primarily addressed – anxiety symptoms are secondary and merely an expression of this inadequate sense of self. In order to move forward I suggest a two-pronged approach: meeting with the parents in order to support them to positively influence their daughter's lifespace dynamics and meeting with Colleen to begin to neutralise her anxious experience. All agree to this initial starting point, though a few days later I receive an

DOI: 10.4324/9781003373599-16

email from Margaret to say that Colleen will come to my office but is insisting that her mum be present during the session.

Parent Strategy Work

My intentions in meeting with these parents are to demystify their daughter's presentation and to develop a more attuned repertoire of responses. Margaret and Bernard arrive at my office eager to hear how I am going to tackle the anxiety and instil resilience in their teenage child. Dad has brought with him a notebook and pen to jot down my expert wisdom and instructions. This couple are demonstrating the intuitive parenting response when anxiety is present in a child's life – they need to *do* something. They have been trying and failing to effect change and now their hope lies in the therapist being able to *do* something. Not surprisingly, therapists commonly experience pressure to *deliver the goods* in these situations, subsequently feeling deskilled and undervalued when they fail to instantly make anxiety symptoms vanish. From the outset, it is important to shift this expectation because the anxiety is much more likely to recede in response to *being* not doing.

I start by indicating to the parents that the questions they have been asking themselves are the wrong questions: *How do we get her to stop being anxious? How do we get her back to school? How do we get her to stop having panic attacks? How do we stop the OCD?* This immediately generates curiosity and self-reflection and begins the shift to a new understanding and new approach. Eradicating symptoms will not necessarily neutralise an inhibitive lifespace, so rather than focusing on how to help rid Colleen of this terrible affliction, there are some more useful questions to consider. I tell them that the bigger issue at stake is that their daughter has no faith in herself – this is precisely *why* she feels anxious. Both parents are interested, and heads are nodding. We explore the adolescent's presentation in more depth during this meeting, which moves to a focus on the parents' experience of their daughter's inhibitive configuration style. As the tone of our conversation becomes more reflective Margaret and Bernard begin to explore their roles and quality of contact within their daughter's lifespace. I shape the dialogue and interventions through this new lens, framing it through some more attuned questions to ponder:

Q1.   How do you enable the comfort zone?

As they describe Colleen's need to feel comfort, I invite the parents to reflect on how they facilitate this, explaining that parenting strategies tend to merely be short-term oxytocin generators which lack transformative potential, for example, reassuring hugs and treats to cheer her up. As the dialogue unfolds both parents begin to appreciate how their contact with the adolescent fosters dependency. The more Colleen struggles the more the parents steps in to compensate, reassure, encourage and indulge. Whilst attempting to be as supportive to their daughter as possible, they begin to realise that continual recycling through this fixed relational theme is not only unhelpful but also reinforces dependency. As Margaret and Bernard recognise the redundancy of their efforts the seeds are sown for them to embrace a new way of being.

Q2.   What happens at the edge of the comfort zone?

Next, a discussion of the adolescent's anxiety symptoms zeros in on how both parents respond when Colleen is experiencing anxiety symptoms. Both parents describe a surge of stress for them when this happens, and a strong sense of urgency coupled with powerlessness as they desperately attempt to calm their daughter. They feel overwhelmed and anxious themselves, trying to reassure and focus on the positives. I invite Margaret to give me an example of what this looks like.

Margaret:	*'She's worried every morning about going to school. I tell her that there's no need to be worried – that she'll be fine. And when it's time to get into my car for the school run, she gets very uptight. I say that there's nothing to be afraid of and school isn't going to do her one bit of harm. If she would just stop worrying and try to be positive, it would make her life far easier. I'm always telling her that it's all in her head and to stop listening to those old thoughts.'*
Therapist:	*'Does that help?'*
Margaret:	*'Not really to be honest. But when she gets home from school, I'll say to her "you see, it wasn't that bad at all now was it?" and give her a bit of confidence that she can do these things.'*
Therapist:	*'And do you see her becoming more confident and struggling less with the morning routine then?'*
Margaret:	*'She's getting worse if anything. Sometimes we end up rowing, she gets mad with me when I'm trying to help. You can't look at her sideways most mornings.'*
Bernard:	*'She'll text or video call me at work if her and Margaret have had a fight in the morning. I try to tell her that her mother's only trying to help. I have to be away early for work so I can't really help. I don't know what to do. I feel useless a good bit of the time.'*
Therapist:	*'It sounds like there are times when your parenting strategy ends up getting everybody stressed. Would it be fair to say that it's not working the way you would like it to?'*
Margaret:	*'Definitely.'*
Bernard:	*'That would be right enough.'*

I remind the parents that they are the most significant and influential people in their daughter's life and that finding effective ways to support Colleen when she is off-balance will make a considerable impact. I explain why they are not making headway with their current approach: when Colleen's comfort zone is under threat her amygdala takes over. Her brain shifts from being dominated by cerebral cortex activity and enters survival mode. This means that the adolescent has moved into an experience of danger, having been triggered into an exaggerated emotional reaction. The adolescent's capacity to reason has left the building and she is in an irrational frame of mind. It is at this point that the parents step in to soothe, however their responses are misaligned. Margaret and Bernard tend to rely on rationalisations and practical advice which misses the heart of the teenager's experience of being caught in amygdala hijack. Whilst rationalising is a very intuitive, automatic and common response for parents, mum and dad are starting to understand that this approach doesn't work. However, they are so reflexively rational in their contact with Colleen now that they will require a convincing rationale for adopting an alternative approach. This time I ask Bernard for an example of an interaction with his daughter to unpack this further.

Bernard: 'Well she was actually texting back and forth with me there just before we came in here. I'll read you the texts.'

Colleen: Not having a good day. I'm so tired I can't even concentrate.

Dad: Have something to eat at break time and you'll feel better.

Colleen: I can't do this anymore. I'm exhausted.

Dad: It's Thursday, it's nearly the weekend. Have a coffee and it'll perk you up a bit. Do your breathing pet.

Therapist: 'That's a great example of what we've been talking about. Your response is perfectly reasonable and full of sound advice. However, I can hear that you're engaging with Colleen as if she is in a rational place, but she's not; she's in a very emotional place. So, we need to tweak how you both interact with her when she's stressed and off-balance like this.'

As parents are prone to adopting a pragmatic style of supporting anxious teenagers and focusing on what they can *do*, I appeal to this logic and frame the adoption of a more emotionally attuned approach in a mechanistic manner – otherwise my guidance will very likely be lost on them. The purpose is to cultivate a more grounded and attuned way of being in the relationship with their daughter rather than giving them techniques to *do*, although the process will feel like the latter. By feeling that they can actually do something tangible to make a difference generates quite a bit of relief for these parents and they become increasingly engaged. I have found over the years that presenting the delicately nuanced processes of cultivating emotional connection and relational depth in a decidedly two-dimensional, technique-oriented manner is an effective way of harnessing parental pragmatism and creating the required shift. I tell them:

'OK, there are four steps which you will need to take to begin to turn this around and help to bring Colleen out of the amygdala-triggered state as effectively and as quickly as possible. Bernard, you might want to write this down in your notepad.'

Step 1: Practice Empathy

'Start to imagine what the world is like from Colleen's perspective. I mean, from the inside out. Imagine the level of threat she experiences, the dread she feels leaving her comfort zone, the oppression of the world she inhabits. I'm going to suggest that you both spend about ten minutes each day for a couple of weeks simply stepping into her shoes and being her. Then write a paragraph or two afterwards about what the experiment was like and what struck you. Try it for different moments in Colleen's life: school mornings, feeling panic, having very little confidence, being obsessive and compulsive about certain things in her life. Do this for one week, then sit together and compare notes. See what you come up with. And if you wish, you can email me about it. Now I won't have time to respond but I'll certainly read it and we can talk about it next time.'

Step 2: Develop an Ear for The Emotional

'Bernard, if we go back to those texts, we'll see that there is something Colleen was communicating that you might be missing. Anxious teenagers often describe how they are feeling but parents tend to respond with a positive statement or a solution. She said she isn't having a good day, she's tired, she can't do this anymore and she's exhausted. So, if we look at your responses…and bear in mind this is the natural response of most parents…you try to help by suggesting remedies for the tiredness and injecting a bit of hope into your messages. That makes perfect sense and on paper looks like an excellent reply. But remember, she's off-balance and not in a reasonable frame of mind – so your very rational, sensible feedback is not going to land.'

Margaret: *'Is that why she always gets irritated when we're trying to be helpful? She's a wild one for rejecting what you're saying or shouting at you that you're not helping or that you don't understand.'*

Therapist: *'Exactly. You're not reaching her in that moment. She's reacting to the mismatch. She feels misunderstood and a little more alone in her struggle.'*

Bernard: *'So, we've been doing the wrong thing the whole time.'*

Therapist: *'Well, parenting teenagers is really hard, especially when they are very anxious. You do your best, but they don't come with a trouble-shooting guide and how are you meant to know if you're getting it right or not?'*

Bernard: *'You're not wrong there Bronagh.'*

Therapist: *'You know, there's no such thing as the perfect parent. Like I said, you do your best…it's called being human. But there's no doubt that the cornerstone of your parenting is well established – your love for your daughter is immense, that's clear to see. And you are generating as much comfort as you can, which is the obvious and intuitive thing*

	to do. Unfortunately, parents find that their strategies don't go far enough.'
Therapist:	*'So, this next task is to develop an ear for the emotional. When Colleen communicates with either of you, learn to fire up your emotional radar and identify feelings. Try listening out for feelings she's naming or describing, and you'll get to the heart of her experience more directly. Sometimes she'll clearly state them and other times she'll hint at them. For example, those couple of texts earlier this morning. They were full of feelings. It's so easy to miss them because, as parents, you are focused on trying to take away her suffering and make everything better. Again, after conversations with Colleen, it will help if you take a bit of time to note down the feelings you picked up. It will take time and practice. And again, feel free to email me with these reflections. I'll be sure to read them before we meet next time.'*

It's important to keep shame and guilt out of the encounter as far as possible. Speaking generically about the challenges of parenting anxious teenagers and validating their intuitive efforts to date will help create curiosity whilst averting negative self-evaluation.

Step 3: Mirror Back and Name Support

'Mirroring her feelings back to her will help to ground and settle Colleen. Offering solutions, trying to be positive and attempting to fix all have their place, but they are premature if your daughter is still off-balance. You have got to help her find calm and a really effective way to do this is to let her know that you recognise her feeling world. This is empathy and is a great way of creating comfort. It will offer a bridge to reconnection with you again. She'll feel met and much less isolated and alone in her struggle. Then after you've communicated your empathy you simply state that you're there to support her. You don't have to qualify your support, just name it. This mirroring and naming of support seems awfully simple, but it can be powerfully effective. Bernard, I'm going back to that message exchange between yourself and herself this morning. It's relatively straightforward – responding to Colleen you just state the obvious about her feeling world and then remind her that you are a support. Actually, we could experiment with this right now. Bernard, are you open to texting Colleen back again?'

I invite both parents to suggest possible responses and we explore how these might land with the adolescent. Bernard types and sends the first text. Colleen responds almost immediately, and a handful of further responses are collectively constructed:

Dad:	*Colleen, you've been on my mind since you texted earlier. Today seems like it's a really tough day and you just sound drained.*
Colleen:	*I feel like I'm drowning in the deep end of a swimming pool.*

Dad:	*It seems like a lonely place to be.*
Colleen:	*Yeah, I'm just tired of it.*
Dad:	*This is too much for you. Well, I want you to know that I'm here to support you.*
Colleen:	*I know.*
Dad:	*I have your back.*
Colleen:	*Thanks Dad, that means a lot.*
Therapist:	*'Can you both see what happened there?'*
Bernard:	*'Yeah, that definitely seemed to settle her alright.'*
Margaret:	*'You could tell she feels a bit better by the last message.'*
Therapist:	*'Again, like Step 2 it takes time and practice. You're so used to jumping in to reassure and fix and that's going to be a difficult habit to break. Keep the intention in your mind that you want to create a bridge to reconnection. Remember to listen out for the feelings, then mirror them back. Anything else is premature. And again, maybe each of you could email me with an example of an exchange between yourself and Colleen – either one that went well or didn't go well – and we can explore it next time.'*

Step 4: Co-regulate

'Staying with the feelings is effective, but the last step is probably the most important because it will help with the first three. It's a big intervention for neutralising her amygdala and generating calm feelings. You see, when someone becomes amygdala-triggered and highly stressed, their nervous system goes into overdrive and that becomes contagious. You were just describing earlier what happens to you when Colleen is at the edge of her comfort zone and feeling triggered – it elevates your stress levels considerably too. So, you have an off-balance teenager attempting to be calmed by two parents whose nervous systems are now wired. The irony is that when parents try to help, they sometimes actually make things worse, by bringing more stress to the situation.'

Bernard:	*'Can't argue with you there.'*
Therapist:	*'The good news is that a calm nervous system is just as contagious as a dysregulated one. We all know this: have you ever been stressed and preoccupied, then spent some time in the presence of someone who is very calm and zen? We pick up their calm and we're changed by the encounter. That's what you're going to begin to do now. You're going to cultivate calm and then your calm is going to help counterbalance and neutralise Colleen's stress.'*
Margaret:	*'I know what you mean, but how does it work exactly?'*
Therapist:	*'There's a chemical in your daughter's brain called oxytocin which triggers a feeling of comfort when released. It has a calming effect and lowers stress. Comfort is in short supply in your daughter's life*

> *which is why she lives in a small, restricted comfort zone. Trying to be positive and giving her advice won't elevate her oxytocin levels… but being a soothing presence will. Oxytocin-rich contact generates oxytocin release in another person, like when we enjoy a hug from someone we care about.'*

Bernard: *'And how do we do that?'*

Therapist: *'Well, living in our modern world is stress-inducing. Raising an anxious teenager is stress-inducing. There are so many stressors in your lives as parents, so you have to now actively work at reducing your baseline of stress in general and also learn techniques to calm yourself in a moment. You have to cultivate high levels of oxytocin and comfort in yourselves as parents.'*

There follows a discussion about the stress dimension of both parents' lives and practices which will contribute to a calmer sense of presence. I suggest yoga, tai chi, journaling, deep breathing, massage and other relaxing activities. I also suggest that they consider creating a space for ongoing attention to stressors in their lives by engaging in their own personal therapy. I then take them through the process of how to remain calm when Colleen is stressed, describing some techniques such as breathing with awareness, staying in touch with their own body and consciously choosing equanimity over fluster. Following this, we return to the last of the three questions in relation to the anxious lifespace.

Q3.   How do you expand the comfort zone?

Having explored the question of enabling and fostering dependency and discussed parental responses to anxiety symptoms, we now turn our attention to expansion of the comfort zone. I draw the comfort zone again (Figure 12.1) and this time identify the desired end position: Colleen is anxiety-free, confident, resilient, socially centrally located and living her life to the full. I explain to the parents that moving towards this through gentle and gradual levels of expansion is the best way forward.

'There is quite a contrast between where you would like Colleen to be and where she actually is. You can support her to reach the desired end point with a step-by-step approach. Let's say each of these rings that I've drawn outside the comfort zone is a level of expansion – your daughter may need to go through a whole bunch of these levels in order to get to a place of much healthier functioning. How to begin is to focus on Level One…just starting with baby steps. Once Level One has been mastered, we move to Level Two and so on. Expanding the comfort zone in slow, steady degrees is how this will be done. We're already at Level One today with some of these changes you are going to make in how you engage with Colleen. You folks focus on that and we'll meet again in a number of weeks to review how things are going.'

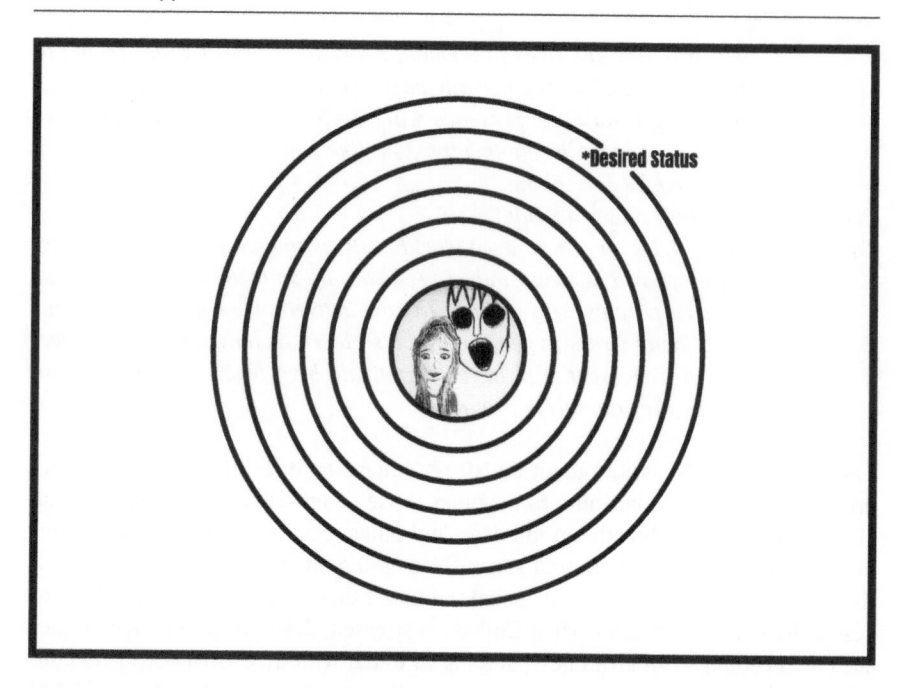

Figure 12.1 Levels of Expansion

During subsequent parent meetings I coach Margaret and Bernard to refine their empathic and regulatory skills. Their emailed reflections will be useful to receive prior to our sessions as there will be rich learning for them in our discussion of these, particularly when things haven't gone well with Colleen. Incidentally, I find that this style of email contact outside of sessions is useful in three ways: it is an effective container for parental anxiety; my boundary of reading but not responding to emails models how to create a receptive holding space without overreaching and having to *do* something; and lastly and most importantly, I am not willing to cut my lunch hour short or spend my evenings answering long-winded emails infused with urgency. I value my free time, though many therapists spend more time in communication with parents outside of session times than they actually do with the adolescent client. I'm not convinced this is helpful to anyone.

As they continue moving through the levels of expansion, I invite the parents to consider a couple of questions when figuring out their next moves: *Is there one thing I can start doing that will help the situation? And one thing I can stop doing?* This active participation is empowering for parents who previously felt overwhelmed and powerless. It is important to support parents to implement realistic expansion of the comfort zone, otherwise their interventions will be way more than Colleen will be able to tolerate. This will set the adolescent up for failure and will end up creating more anxiety. Levels of expansion must be attuned and proportionate.

Soon also in our work together, I will address the adolescent's developing sense of self and how that is being supported and shaped by the parents. This relates to enabling of the comfort zone and external validation. Speaking generically, I will describe how parents tend to find conversations limited to two principal topics when communicating with their inhibitive teen: anxiety and performance. Dialogue about anxiety symptoms, fears, worries, dread and overwhelm is a way to offload and seek comfort. However, it focuses on the negative, on what's not going well and emphasises the young person's struggles. Performance-related talk provokes the adolescent's pressure, fuelling her misguided concept of how to be acceptable. For example, if academic work is discussed, there is every chance that Colleen will project her own internal pressure on to parents and feel that it is her mum or dad who is pressuring her. This will then create even more pressure to succeed and not let adults down. I will support the parents to shift conversation into a more positive mode and identify other topics which won't set off a pressure response. Performance-related communication feeds into the adolescent's external-ised sense of self, reinforcing the belief that outward signs of success such as high grades, trophies or the perfect figure are the pathway to acceptance by others...and if others accept her, then just maybe she will feel a sliver of self-acceptance. This can be a difficult contact pattern to break as it is very often a deeply rooted mode of relatedness between adolescent and parent. This discussion will involve parents noting the themes of dialogue with their daughter and reflecting on how Colleen may internalise this.

Antagonistic Parenting Approaches

In Colleen's case above, her parents Margaret and Bernard are directional, well-balanced individuals. They grasp the concept of the inhibitive lifespace and, with support, begin to understand why they have been disempowered and how they are potentially enabling the adolescent's inhibitive experience. These directional parents have a good sense of self, have the capacity to reflect on their parenting and to remain attuned and strategic. They buy into the therapeutic enterprise because they become aware that there is more at stake than simply getting their teenage child to attend school or stop having panic attacks. The therapist's task is to create a deeper level of receptivity in the parents' way of relating to their daughter and support them to foster in her courage and grit. This quite radical shift in parenting is a challenging task which requires patience and commitment. People who remain entrenched in an impulsive or inhibitive configuration style beyond adolescence and who then become parents themselves tend to struggle when rearing inhibitive adolescents.

The Impulsive Parent

Thirteen-year-old Ben has struggled with anxiety and negative overthinking since childhood. His father Wesley is an impulsive person and prone to reactivity. He is not psychologically minded, but rather a 'man's man' who works hard and tends to overindulge on drink at weekends. He finds it difficult that his son is not interested in farming or soccer. Wesley's relationship with Ben is characterised through discomfort and intolerance. Conversely, he has great rapport with his two older sons who share his interests. There is an ease in their relating and they have much to talk about: cattle, tractors, football matches etc. and the three regularly enjoy trips to England to watch their favourite team play. Ben, on the other hand, loves fashion design, art and drama. His friends are all girls and he very definitely is not a man's man. Wesley views his son as strange and does not know how to communicate with Ben. Dad tends to overlook the adolescent due to his discomfort. Ben's mother Edith has compensated over the years by developing a close connection to the adolescent and by being the comfort parent within his anxious lifespace.

Ben struggles to attend school and has mild OCD which is principally focused on contamination fears such as touching doorknobs and other surfaces. Wesley reacts at times with exasperation or anger when his son insists on staying home from school or in response to the constant hand washing and wiping down of surfaces. Wesley is too busy to attend the initial assessment meeting, though agrees to come to a parent strategy session. Entering a therapist's office is an alien concept to him and his philosophy in life is that *'you just get on with it'*. According to dad, Ben is an attention seeker who manipulates his mother. He tells me that he is always giving out to his wife Edith for being too soft and mollycoddling the boy – she has him ruined and that's where the problem lies. If Ben would just get out and get his hands dirty on the farm, that would do him the world of good. Dad has learned to avoid Ben in the mornings, as he cannot tolerate his son's panic in relation to going to school and is fed up fighting with him. Ben needs to man up. As for the OCD symptoms, this is just ridiculous nonsense.

I manage to create sufficient interest for Wesley to commit to attending some further parental involvement sessions with Edith. These sessions focus on supporting dad to acknowledge his disappointment and shame that Ben is not more like himself and his two other sons. Working on acceptance and validation comes next, however, this is not a straightforward task as Wesley has little tolerance for much of Ben's self-expression and often cannot stop himself from openly insulting the teenager. Dad lacks insight into his son's experience and struggles to empathise with Ben. This creates considerable strain between them, and their relationship is hurtling towards mutual contempt. Sexual orientation and gender identity become figural for the adolescent during therapy, however Wesley's prejudice and propensity to become reactive are amped up significantly as he dismisses the disclosure as *'another attention seeking stunt'* and describes the adolescent as *'always having to be different'*. Dad blames his wife, Ben's activities and friends, and social media for *'putting the boy's head astray'*. It is virtually impossible to support Wesley to make the necessary adjustments to his parenting in order to support Ben's lifespace expansion, such is his lack of self-reflective capacity, empathy and emotional containment. The adolescent has learned not to absorb his father's hostility and is flourishing, not because of, but in spite of, this parent.

The Inhibitive Parent

Seventeen-year-old Jade struggles with anxiety and social interaction. She is very shy and feels academically and socially pressured at school. Her parents, Catherine and Mike, run a successful business and are self-confessed workaholics, spending long hours in the office or travelling. These parents are inhibitive and have both developed an externalised sense of self. Their pragmatic approach to parenting means that their focus is on supporting their children to *do* well in life. Their emphasis is on productivity and performance: good grades, sporting achievement, neat presentation and central social location. Prioritising outward signs of flourishing means that emotional development and validation have not been nurtured in their children's lives.

Jade had always been a sensitive child and due to the family culture, this aspect of her experience had not been well supported. She asked to see a therapist repeatedly during her earlier adolescence, recognising that she had a serious problem with talking to people and felt completely unconfident in the world. These requests were always deflected by the parents: *'What need would you have to see a therapist? Sure, don't you have everything you could want?'* When Jade opened up to either parent about her struggles, they brushed off her experience with comments such as, *'I was like that myself when I was your age'* or *'You'll grow out of it.'* The established family culture is deflective humour and the adolescent's intensity is, more often than not, met with light-hearted banter. An unspoken family rule of engagement is 'we don't do feelings'.

As the adolescent's anxiety symptoms worsens, her level of emotional distress and frustration at her parents' responses intensifies and finally she starts self-harming. Following a phone call from the school upon discovery of fresh forearm scars, the parents make an appointment with me. Their discomfort at being in my office is subtly evident. Catherine expresses indignation that her daughter has self-harmed, *'We work so hard to give her a good life, and this is how she repays us.'* Mum demonstrates some narcissistic tendencies and I sense that Mike is mildly resentful that his attendance at meetings adds pressure to his already over-committed schedule. He has more important things to do. Whilst mum and dad appear confident and engaging, they are at a loss when I field feelings-related questions during our meetings. I have a sense that I hardly know them after several months of ongoing contact. Parenting strategy work feels almost fruitless as they tend to minimise their daughter's struggles and just don't get the purpose of interventions. When I suggest that Jade's presentation may warrant assessment for autism, they strongly disagree and let me know that assessment is out of the question. They favour a quick fix and do not want Jade's medical record tarnished with a diagnosis of this kind.

As I meet the adolescent, Jade feels immediately relieved to be able to open up to someone about her experience. She tells me, *'I've basically felt like shit for most of my life and my parents don't seem to notice.'* The adolescent feels deeply overlooked by her parents despite their great love for her and their considerable efforts to parent responsibly. In order for Mike and Catherine to demonstrate the depth of emotional attunement, openness and understanding required to be fully receptive to Jade, this would necessitate engagement in intensive personal therapy in order to develop a strong sense of self and reflective relationship to their parenting. I doubt this is likely given their entrenched inhibitive configuration styles and sceptical attitude towards therapy.

Chapter 13

Therapy with the Inhibitive Adolescent – One-to-one Work

Impulsive adolescents wouldn't dream of having a parent join them in a session and usually want their parents as far removed from the process as possible. Not so with inhibitive young people. It is quite common for anxious teens to request that a comfort parent stays with them during therapeutic work which the therapist has intended as specifically one-to-one work. This can be off-putting for some therapists who may object or feel stressed that a parent will be observing. However, these situations should be embraced for a couple of reasons: joint participation will afford the parent an opportunity to understand and appreciate their teenager's lifespace dynamics more fully; and if adolescents feel threatened within the therapeutic space, they will become passive and voiceless. Most adolescent therapists are familiar with the muted, shoulder-shrugging client who is unable to initiate dialogue and whom they then set about interrogating in a question-answer-question-answer fashion. The young person's answers tend to be limited to monosyllabic responses and excessive use of the phrase *'I don't know'*. The therapist ends up doing all the work and her feelings of frustration are a response to the adolescent's experience of discomfort. The therapeutic space becomes infused with subtle, unspoken pressure and it can feel like doing therapy with a ragdoll. Therefore, involving the parent fully, if this is requested by the adolescent, is important. However, supporting mum or dad to step back at a timely point may also be necessary and beneficial.

Colleen and Margaret arrive at my office for the first in-person appointment. Mum and I say hello though the adolescent neither makes eye contact nor responds to my greeting. I open by addressing Colleen, knowing that she is unlikely to step out of her passive posture.

Therapist: *'It's good to see you in person. How have you been since me met online a few weeks ago?'*
Colleen looks at mum. Mum looks at Colleen. The adolescent bows her head.
Mum: *'Well Bronagh, we've had a bad few weeks, I'm not going to lie. We weren't able to manage school a few days last week. Now we did have a good weekend I must say, but Monday morning didn't go well. And we've been very anxious, not able to leave the bedroom much. We had*

DOI: 10.4324/9781003373599-17

one or two meltdowns too, didn't we pet? But we're focusing on the positives and we're trying very hard.'

I think to myself, *Who in heaven's name are you talking about Margaret? Don't you mean to say that Colleen had a bad few weeks?...not you?...that Monday morning didn't go well for her?...that she wasn't able to leave the bedroom much and had a couple of meltdowns?* This identity fusion which so often happens between an anxious adolescent and their comfort parent means that the parent almost becomes an extension of the teenager. Margaret has become her daughter's voice beyond the comfort zone, such is the level of Colleen's dependency. I note the use of terms of endearment such as pet, darling or sweetie which interestingly I hear parents use much less frequently when addressing either impulsive or directional teens. This opening dialogue point is precisely why it is useful to involve parents and not object to their participation when meeting with the young person. Supporting an adolescent without attending to the parent's contact style of fostering dependency in an attempt to provide comfort may well turn into a fruitless enterprise.

As our conversation progresses, my experience tells me that relying on the verbal alone will not support the adolescent either to participate richly or to integrate meaning and interventions. Colleen's hyper-rational, negatively self-referenced lens presents a somewhat distorted perspective of herself and her world. I want to promote frontal lobe activation with access to bigger-picture thinking, a more realistic viewpoint and, of course, resilience. Using *Sandspace*, we begin to tentatively co-sculpt the adolescent's lifespace (Figure 13.1). Portrayed is a small comfort zone within which is her home, her parents and herself on a screen. The edge of the comfort zone consists of artefacts representing her anxiety symptoms, fears and negative body preoccupation. Beyond the comfort zone are some of the dimensions of her lifespace which feel threatening to Colleen, including relating to peers, school attendance and academic work, music performance which she loved prior to lockdown and which she has now given up, death, going to college and her future. Margaret's presence in the therapeutic space is very helpful during this process. Inviting both to reflect on dimensions of the adolescent's experience includes Colleen, so she does not feel she is being 'talked about'. At the same time, it takes the pressure off her to actively engage and permits mum to participate in the dialogue without shame or power struggling. As the adolescent's lifespace narrative is visually represented I am on the lookout for fragments of contact with Colleen.

Being so fixated on perceived threats from people, places and things outside the comfort zone means that the adolescent's capacity to engage in logical reasoning or feel excitement and joy is seriously undermined. It is evident that practically everything outside the comfort zone has become a pressure point and this teenager is caught in a world of overthinking, expectation, frustration, overwhelm and collapse. I offer my observation that Colleen's cognitive bandwidth is greatly compromised which is bound to be creating enormous mental drain.

Figure 13.1 Colleen's Anxious Lifespace

Therapist:	*'As I look at this representation of your life in the sand, I'm really struck by how oppressive everything must be for you.'*
Colleen:	*'Yeah.'*
Therapist:	*'Mum, what do you think it's like for Colleen to live in this oppressive lifespace?'*
Margaret:	*'I think it's very difficult for the wee pet. It must be a nightmare.'*
Therapist:	*'Is your mum right? Is it a nightmare?'*
Colleen:	*'Yeah.'*
Therapist:	*'Colleen, can you give me three words that come to mind when you step back and see your life from this perspective?'*
Colleen:	*'Bad. Stuck…. I don't know.'*
Therapist:	*'Well, bad and stuck are pretty powerful words. I find it a little hard to breathe when you say stuck…that's a tough and lonely place to be.'*
Colleen:	*'Yeah.'*

Over subsequent sessions, dialogue continues to support the unfolding of the lifespace narrative, and more critically to acknowledge and validate the adolescent's subjective experience. Colleen is unable to actively and directly give voice to much of her experience though respectful, tentative and empathic offering of hunches and generic normalisings go a long way to affirming her experience. This empathic bridging, almost imperceptibly at first, brings Colleen's voice online and she increasingly joins the dialogue as an active participant. In a short time, she will outgrow the need to have Margaret by her side during our meetings.

With anxious adolescents, the initial phase of therapy involves no effort or movement on the part of the client. No interventions are offered, and no suggestions made. This will only bombard the therapeutic space with pressure and likely set the young person up for failure. The central focus is *bridging*, that is, understanding, bearing witness, empathising and actively validating in order to establish safe, meaningful contact. An important message communicated to the adolescent is that she doesn't have to *do* anything to be acceptable here; she just has to *be*. This is potentially a profoundly novel experience which may simultaneously disarm and relieve the young person. This approach can also engender urgency for some therapists who may feel that they ought to be *doing* something and getting results. Modelling presence rather than getting results is a powerful antidote to inhibitive functioning and is, in itself, a healing balm.

Colleen's bewilderment diminishes as she literally and metaphorically gets the picture of how her lifespace has become organised. She feels validated and more understood by her parents. She is engaging in a richer and more voiceful manner with me. Mum now sits in the waiting room during sessions. But…is the adolescent ready for change? As the work progresses, two important therapeutic considerations naturally emerge as we approach a choice point for the client.

My first pondering has to do with the extent of acceptance and humanity the adolescent affords herself. If self-judgement and shame are pronounced, I take this as a sign that there is insufficient support for transformation. We stay with the unfolding process and do not proceed to active intervention work. The aim of this paradoxical approach to change is to affect an attitude shift and a heightening of compassion within the client for her predicament. I determine that whilst Colleen is progressing well, her understanding and self-perception need more support. I sit deeply into the therapeutic space and attend to how our relational connectedness and my empathic resonance is influencing the adolescent's meaning making. I trust that rich therapeutic presence will sow the seeds for change by infusing the space with acceptance, potentially prompting a more balanced frontal lobe-dominated mode of meaning-making and newly integrated understanding.

The second consideration relates to the client's level of motivation to change. It is tempting for therapists to roll their sleeves up and get to the 'doing' part of therapy, however prematurity of intervention is a major pitfall in the work with adolescent clients. So many therapists introduce wonderful interventions which ordinarily would work splendidly, but which have been prematurely timed and have subsequently landed like a lead balloon. This disheartening work engenders frustration and client-blaming for less experienced therapists: *she doesn't want to help herself.* It is prudent to secure a collaborative alliance where the young person feels the stirring of motivation to reconfigure their lifespace. If this is not evident, it is useful to create a non-shaming dilemma for the client outlining the bind they are in.

Therapist:	*'You seem miserable and I see how much you are struggling. At the same time, you seem hesitant and fearful about exploring other possibilities. That's quite a dilemma for you.'*
Colleen:	*'Yeah.'*
Therapist:	*'I imagine it's a really tough place to be. You really are stuck, aren't you?'*
Colleen:	*'Yeah.'*
Therapist:	*'It seems to me Colleen that you feel threatened much of the time without knowing what steps to take to meet the danger.'*
Colleen:	*'Yeah.'*
Therapist:	*'The thing is that I think I could help…but I'm not sure that you're open to it.'*
Colleen:	*'Maybe.'*
Therapist:	*'If I had a pill right now that gave you the courage to be out in the world with faith in yourself, going to school every day, being able to talk to people with ease…would you swallow it?'*
Colleen:	*'I'm not sure. Probably not.'*
Therapist:	*'It strikes me that you are so used to living in the comfort zone that freedom and joy and confidence feel almost alien to you.'*
Colleen:	*'Yeah, I don't think I really know how to be happy anymore.'*
Therapist:	*'That's a big statement. What's it like to say that you're not sure you know how to be happy anymore?'*
Colleen:	*'I don't know.'*
Therapist:	*'Well, I figure your happiness has something to do with changing up this comfort zone and I think I get how threatening that feels for you. So, happiness maybe feels a little scary.'*
Colleen:	*'I never thought about it like that before, but yeah, maybe.'*
Therapist:	*'So, are we OK to not make changes for another while?'*
Colleen:	*'Yeah.'*

When I think of therapy with adolescents, I imagine us walking together. If we are equally paced and walking shoulder to shoulder, or better still if the adolescent is a step or two in front, that's great. However, when the therapist is even half a footstep further on or powering ahead, dragging the client along, there is imbalance and power struggling within the therapeutic relationship and therapy is 'being done' to the client. Sitting with the trepidation and disorientation which lifespace expansion may create is a necessary step in readying the adolescent to embrace change. At all times the therapist's contact is accepting and validating, which in itself is a powerful antidote to the young person's inadequate and unacceptable sense of self. I hold in mind that I am not so much trying to eradicate anxiety symptoms as support the reconfiguration of the adolescent's lifespace.

Before long, Colleen's curiosity gradually starts to give way to tentative courage and motivation. We are now ready to experiment with active interventions.

I explain that simply figuring a way to reduce OCD symptoms or panic attacks, or even the overthinking, isn't going to solve the issue at hand. A radical reshaping of the lifespace is required in which the comfort zone is expanded, thus neutralising threat and reducing the intensity of anxiety symptoms. This is a three-stage process.

Calming the Adolescent's Nervous System

Colleen is relieved to learn that this initial stage does not require her to leave her comfort zone at all. I explain to her that there is insufficient oxytocin – a comfort chemical – in her life and we need to create it in abundance (other neurochemicals and brain processes are also involved in creating a feeling of comfort and sooth- ing, though the adolescent hasn't come to my office for a neuroscience lesson, and so we keep concepts simple and straightforward). At present, Colleen's oxytocin intake tends to be passive and comes from parental reassurance and hugs, being with her dog and watching movies. Active engagement in this process will result in two things: additional oxytocin and some much needed lifespace momentum that will be harnessed later on. We explore and she experiments with some possibilities. Top of the bill is developing a regular home practice of yoga which calms the body and refocuses the mind. I share with her my clinical observation from supporting thousands of kids over two and a half decades: young people who demonstrate a willingness to commit to a daily yoga practice do better and stay better. She's will- ing to give it a go, and the beauty of yoga is that it requires only a mat and some floor space. There are tons of online resources and the adolescent will not have to panic about attending a class and drowning in self-conscious discomfort, if that feels too much for her. Other suggestions include mindful breathing, singing in the shower, tapping (a type of acupressure) and getting barefoot in nature. Calming her nervous system means that the adolescent will reach the edge of her comfort zone less rapidly and less automatically. Daily commitment to increasing her oxytocin levels will act as a circuit breaker. It is prudent to remain at this stage until there is evidence of developmental momentum, that is to say, until the adolescent has begun to actively engage in this enterprise. Half-hearted attempts inevitably result in premature intervention and collapse.

Developing the Inner Neuroscientist

Generating oxytocin is about cultivating new ground, and when the adolescent learns the art of self-regulation, she will also have more access to logic. Next the hostile voice of toxic self-criticism requires challenge and containment. Colleen's self-derisory inner dialogue defeats her and she has no counter for it. An alterna- tive, kinder, more reality-based self-talk needs to take hold. I start this process by embodying the hostile voice and exploiting the adolescent's care for her younger sister in order to begin development of an alternative perspective.

'*Let's say I become your hostile voice. I follow you around for the next week, shadowing your every move. I sit beside you in school, show up when you're with people and talk to you the way you talk to yourself. I stand at your shoulder and whisper things into your ear all day long: "you are so pathetic and stupid; people think you're an idiot; you look disgusting – so fat and ugly; I can't believe you showed up looking like that today; why did you say that it sounds so ridiculous?; don't even bother studying for that exam because you're going to fail – that's all you ever do".'*

I don't hold back because Colleen's self-derisory voice doesn't hold back. This is precisely how she talks to herself. The next part of this intervention supports the adolescent to view this self-directed hostility from a more objective stance.

Therapist:	*'You know Colleen, if I actually did just that and said those things, it wouldn't take too long before it became too hard to bear. It would feel like emotional and mental abuse.'*
Colleen:	*'Yeah.'*
Therapist:	*'We're both agreed then – it would feel abusive. And it makes me sad to think that it's not someone else doing this to you – which would be a terrible thing – but that you're doing it to yourself. What's it like to think that you are emotionally and mentally abusing yourself?... because that's what this is.*
Colleen:	*'I wouldn't go that far.'*
Therapist:	*'OK, so let's take your little sister. How about you start turning your hostile voice on her and saying the things you say to yourself to Aine instead?'*
Colleen:	*'I couldn't do that.'*
Therapist:	*'Oh?'*
Colleen:	*'OK I get it, but I don't know how to stop doing it.'*
Therapist:	*'Are you willing to experiment?'*
Colleen:	*'Yeah.'*
Therapist:	*'Great. What's going on is that your brain is doing its best, but it's still developing and connecting. It's not fully online yet, so your thinking is filtered in a way that makes you feel insecure and bad about yourself sometimes. Your hostile voice is just a bad habit, that's all.'*
Colleen:	*'So, it's just my adolescent brain throwing itself out the window?'*
Therapist:	*'I guess you could say that.'*

I support Colleen to start thinking of the hostile inner narrative in an objective way – as a phenomenon of her developing brain, rather than as a true statement of who she is. This cultivates an observing posture and my hope is that the adolescent will stop personalising and start objectifying this neurotic tendency. I frame it simply as her still-developing and not quite fully mature and interconnected cerebral cortex being stuck in a groove. Rather than challenge the actual thoughts (because that tends to feel like an insurmountable challenge to a lot of inhibitive adolescents) we simply figure out ways to bring the frontal lobe online. I explain to her that human beings can learn the discipline of being choiceful about where they direct their attention. Right now, negative self-absorption is consuming her attentional bandwidth – not because the thoughts are true or helpful, but because that's what happens when the cerebral cortex is still maturing and not fully online. This interpretation of Colleen's self-deprecation and hostile overthinking as a brain chemistry issue, rather than a true reflection of who she is, helps her to develop a more objective, observing lens. She starts to consider that perhaps her inner dialogue is, in actual fact, a distorted representation both of herself and her world. Frontal lobe activation will begin to overwrite the massive negative feedback loop which holds the adolescent hostage.

Playfully, we cultivate Colleen's 'inner neuroscientist' where she adopts a posture of curiosity rather than confrontation or collapse. Aware now that her still-developing cerebral cortex is in overdrive again, she choicefully redirects her attention to other things. Every adolescent finds particular things which work best for them. Colleen discovers that the diving reflex (submerging her face in ice-cold water), tapping, yoga, loving kindness meditation and skipping whilst doing mental arithmetic out loud are surprisingly effective antidotes to the ruminating. Psychologically this is no small feat – the adolescent is transitioning from passive to active participation in her life. The transformative effect is significant – Colleen's repertoire of feelings has increased from the dread, fear and sadness she had endured for so long. The sense of relief and empowerment in developing increasing mastery over her unbridled and relentless negative thought process creates hope which opens her to excitement and joy. Nevertheless, this is a tough and ongoing exercise as Colleen reflexively returns to self-criticism and hyper-cautious insecurity again and again. This psychological habit is a well-formed neural pathway for the adolescent.

Levels of Expansion

Next, we begin to experiment with tiptoeing out of the comfort zone. In truth, we have already begun the process of expanding the comfort zone with all that the adolescent has accomplished up until now. I visually depict the levels of expansion using *Sandspace* (Figure 12.1) and point out to Colleen that in order to become the confident, self-possessed young woman she would like to be, baby steps are a safe and sure way of getting there. Right now, there are so many things she feels unable to do, so many fears she feels unable to conquer. I remind Colleen that whilst she can't do everything, she can do *some* things. We begin at Level One and the adolescent selects three manageable tasks to work on at a time – one from each category of people, places and things. As developmental momentum is stirring and the new parental approach is complementing these levels of expansion, the process tends to unfold relatively smoothly.

With regard to places, Colleen chooses to sit at the dinner table with her family one evening a week instead of taking her dinner to her room. For the things category, she opts to put her phone on her bedroom windowsill at night, out of reach and with notifications turned off so that it might help her sleep. I sometimes make suggestions though it is important that the young person remains choiceful in relation to this experience and that tasks are not decided upon or thrust on her as this will promote and enable passivity and failure.

The Deconstruction of Friendship

Like so many inhibitive adolescents, Colleen is at a loss in relation to people. Over the years I have watched many young people suffer the terrible pain of social isolation. They stand on the periphery of the peer world and have no idea how to belong as their attempts so often end in failure and rejection. So, I have figured out a staged approach to the high stakes enterprise of making friends which makes it more accessible and achievable for adolescents. First, I outline the stages to Colleen, then we can make a plan.

Stage 1: Reaching Out

'You're walking along the school corridor and pass another student who seems nice. You wouldn't mind being friends with them. There are four options: you walk straight on and don't acknowledge them; you neutrally acknowledge them by nodding your head; you make eye contact and smile warmly; you make eye contact, smile warmly and say their name. The first two give no indication whatsoever to the other person that you are at all interested in making contact. The third is much better, but the final option gives a clear message to the person: "hey, I'm nice and friendly and approachable and I'm up for friendship".'

Colleen admits that her typical posture is to avoid contact with anyone outside her comfort zone. I make a suggestion that she chooses one person each day to reach out to – perhaps someone she sits beside in class or someone she would quite like to be friends with. Together we come up with ideas about how she might do the reaching out. It may begin as non-verbal then move to dialogic relating: making eye contact, warmly smiling and calling people by their name, asking about something they're interested in. We include reaching out via social media also, as this can be a helpful step given that it is a powerful social landscape for adolescents. I encourage the adolescent to ensure that contact does not take the form of interrogation and tell her to aim for a 50/50 balance in the conversation. We make a list of potential conversation starters. The point is to support Colleen to begin actively engaging other peers in reciprocal dialogue characterised by mutuality rather than dependence.

Stage 2: Familiarity

'The reaching out takes quite a bit of effort – you're trying to think of things to say and it might not always feel that comfortable…but you keep going taking small

steps. A tiny moment of reaching out each day is sometimes all that's required. Then before too long it starts getting a little easier. You'll find that it's not so effortful talking to some of the people you're reaching out to. You're not friends yet; you're just becoming more familiar with one another.'

Stage 3: Friendliness

'You keep committing to reaching out and the familiarity begins to move into friendliness. You're still not friends, but the effort to show up and reach out gets less and less. You start to relax and stop spending your time trying to figure out what to say or second-guessing yourself. Your goal is to create a bank of friendliness: to develop a friendly relationship with as many people as feels good for you.'

Stage 4: Friendship

'You can't force friendships to form. There's just a chemistry that happens and the friendliness you develop with a small handful of people will naturally and organically morph into friendship. When that happens, it's wonderful if those friends are a good fit. Some people are naturally gifted at this – they just show up and almost instantly they proceed through the four stages in the blink of an eye...but lots of people have to work at it. And the thing is, if you don't reach out, you'll never have friends. Remember too that sometimes friendships don't work out, so if you have restricted yourself exclusively to one or two friends and that falls apart, you're back to isolation and loneliness. It's a good idea to keep nurturing your bank of friendliness where you keep reaching out to others and staying friendly. That means if friendships go sour, you're just back to stage three, not stage one.'

I remind Colleen that it takes the courage of a lion to reach out. I encourage her not to focus on having friends but rather on developing a friendly rapport with peers. Making friends can feel like a bewildering impossibility for inhibitive adolescents, however deconstructing the art of making friends into concrete and coherent stages tends to demystify the process and make it feel manageable. Colleen is delighted with herself as the reaching out soon starts to pay off. Peer belonging and meaningful friendships make a monumental difference to any adolescent and help considerably to expand the comfort zone.

I continue to support the adolescent's calming of her nervous system and development of the inner neuroscientist whilst also attending to the gradual reconfiguration of the inhibitive lifespace through workable levels of comfort zone expansion. Focusing on her present-day experience and learning to tolerate uncertainty about the future is liberating for the adolescent. Colleen's emotional, behavioural and social development steadily extends as her internal resistance to experiencing life is replaced by faith in herself and her world. It is not possible for human beings, and maybe especially adolescents, to live anxiety-free lives. The therapist's role is to support them to keep moving in the right direction.

The Challenge of Entrenched Inhibition

Some adolescents are caught in an entrenched inhibitive configuration style to such a rigid degree that the possibility of extending their comfort zone feels insurmountable. Ciara was a shy child with a small friendship circle who was prone to worrying and a little rigid in her ways. She was a competitive swimmer and a successful gymnast who didn't particularly enjoy school but managed fine. However, at fourteen years of age, her low-grade anxiety seemed to explode, and the adolescent received a diagnosis of autism. For the next few years, Ciara found life tough going.

Now in her senior year, Ciara misses a lot of school and mornings are particularly stressful for everyone. She hates being wakened by her mum or dad and there is usually an argument. Ciara protests that if her parents would simply back off, she would be fine. However, when left to her own devices, she sleeps for most of the day. Ciara maintains a connection with her three childhood friends, though the friendship does not extend beyond the school gates. The adolescent is often invited to social gatherings with them, though she convinces herself that they are 'only being nice' and don't really want her to come along, so she always declines. The adolescent's level of self-directed hostility is intense and exhausting. She likes nothing about herself and constantly feels inadequate. The effort to mask in school leaves her drained. By the time she arrives home each evening, Ciara feels overwhelmed and is easily triggered into aggressive outbursts with family members. Her parents' hunch is that Ciara actively seeks conflict in order to let off steam after accumulating stress throughout the school day. The adolescent resists any requests or advice from her parents and is in a constant power struggle with them. She rejects their encouragement and finds it difficult to accept their support.

Ciara's relationship to food and exercise has become increasingly ritualised and inflexible, characterised by a restrictive and nutrient deficient diet, with gym sessions to manage the guilt of eating and fear of gaining weight. The adolescent has also developed OCD symptoms and engages in self-harming behaviour. Ciara spends most of the time in her room rewatching her favourite shows or studying. She is naturally academic and predicted to do very well in her A level exams. The idea of school ending fills her with relief, however she feels very stressed at the thought of embarking on a college course with all the social, emotional and other general upheaval this will mean for her.

Change is very problematic for Ciara who feels that her life is merely a process of negotiating and, if possible, avoiding the ubiquitous pressures and challenges she meets each day. The adolescent feels miserable and utterly exhausted much of the time, with toxic self-dialogue and micro-analysis of situations relentlessly playing out in her head. The greater the stress, the more self-destructive her creative adjustments become and the more despondent the adolescent feels. She recognises that the rigid eating behaviours, the vomiting, the cutting and the angry outbursts are limiting and unhelpful – they bother and disgust her a lot. The dilemma for Ciara, however, is that paradoxically they also generate relief and calm.

Therapy is helpful for Ciara as the empathic attunement creates relief and calm too, though unlike most of her typical stress-reducing strategies, this mode offers her a constructive way of experiencing it. Our conversations support her self-understanding as the adolescent begins to make meaning of her autistic presentation. And whilst Ciara develops impressive insight into her lifespace dynamics and finds her voice with me, our predicament is that her comfort zone and symptoms have become entrenched. She feels threatened at the idea of relinquishing them and she is unwilling to experiment. This counterintuitive posture is very strong and Ciara herself says, *'I know it sounds crazy, but this is who I am and I'm not changing.'* After three weeks of college Ciara drops out and returns home to the comfort of her familiar lifespace, utterly overwhelmed. Our work remains at the supportive level for some time until tiny glimmers of flexibility and expansion appear, and she starts to make slow but steady progress.

Chapter 14

Therapy with the Directional Adolescent

There is a different quality to therapeutic work with directional adolescents than with young people who are impulsively or inhibitively configured. The principal distinction is that their configuration style itself is not problematic and does not become a focus of therapeutic intervention. Anxious or depressive symptoms tend to be a natural response to environmental stressors and are not character driven.

Let's take three adolescents who are referred for therapy because of a sexual assault. The impulsive adolescent's developmental location will need to be addressed in order for them to be able to process the trauma: namely their lack of self-reflective capacity, their propensity for risk-taking and their lack of emotional containment. These will all potentially thwart the adolescent's progress and so ongoing intervention tends to target these traits as developmental work precedes and supports trauma processing for these adolescents. Similarly, the primary therapeutic consideration for the inhibitive adolescent who presents having endured sexual violence is how the experience has reinforced the comfort zone and exacerbated anxiety symptoms. For both these adolescents, supporting them to become a client in the first instance and developing the necessary psychological and developmental resources to work through traumatic experiences are the immediate challenges. Therapists who work in rape crisis centres are familiar with this scenario – they offer a specialist service, though commonly end up undertaking developmental work with adolescent clients. Conversely, the directional adolescent who presents because of having been sexually assaulted has developed a good degree of psychological, emotional and relational stability. This translates as the adolescent having a certain deal of self-discipline, courage and equanimity. For sure, the young person may creatively adjust to the trauma in an impulsive or inhibitive fashion, however it is just that – a response to traumatic suffering. Their symptoms are not developmental in nature. This adolescent shows up to therapy as a willing participant and can hold their own in the dialogue. One notable aspect in working with directional adolescents is that the therapist does not have to do all the work. There is a quality of mutuality in the contact which can make it feel like therapy with an adult client. It is very definitely not, as adulthood is still a long way off, developmentally speaking.

DOI: 10.4324/9781003373599-18

It's probably safe to say that no one has ever sought out therapy for a frontal lobe-activated young person for purely developmental reasons such as battles with parents, 'attitude' problems, an anxious lifespace or crippling self-doubt. Their presentation, even if it is a creative adjustment to adversity and a statement of having to be self-reliant, tends to give the adult world less cause for concern than their impulsive or inhibitive counterparts. Directional adolescents commonly make their way to therapy because of indirect issues where people or experiences within their lifespace are creating concern or distress. Instances include parental separation, bereavement or having endured a trauma such as in the previous example. These young people also sometimes identify issues which they feel are important to process such as their adoption or dynamics which emerge in intimate relationships. (My previous publication *Adolescence: A Radical Relational Approach* offers guidance to clinicians on specific clinical presentations and details relational intervention styles.)

Sometimes frontal lobe-activated adolescents show up simply looking for space and support to tease out future direction or some other aspect of their experience which is causing uncertainty. Family process is possibly the most common referral reason for directional adolescents who tend to feel somewhat overlooked and neglected. Shouldering the responsibility of being a parentified adolescent can create a feeling of being lost inside and of not living life on one's own terms. For these adolescents, very often the experience of being in the presence of a safe, attentive, validating adult is all the healing they need, and any formal intervention work is secondary. Therapy is about creating a space in the world for their light to shine. One directional adolescent who lives in a relatively chaotic family in which his needs are low on the pecking order admits openly that he does not need to come to therapy, but simply values the support and is just *'working through kinks'*. He doesn't need help; he needs to be seen and heard.

At times, typically resourceful and thriving adolescents enter therapy with gradual or sudden onset of anxious or depressive symptoms. This may seem quite mystifying to everyone, though there is nearly always a reasonable context which makes sense of their presentation. Twenty-three-year-old Juliette is the youngest of a family of five girls. Her parents separated when she was seven and since then she has rarely had contact with her father who was psychologically and physically abusive to his wife. Over the years the girls, one by one, left home to study and, as the youngest, Juliette remains at home with her mother, Shirley. The adolescent's four older sisters now live in England, Canada and Australia. Juliette requests to see me because she is feeling depressed. Her boyfriend has recently ended their relationship and she has been putting on weight. The adolescent feels that she has lost her confidence. To make matters worse, most of Juliette's friends have moved away from home and she finds herself lonely and at a loss for interesting things to do or people to do them with. Juliette works in a local hotel as a receptionist and whilst she is glad to have a job and finds it relatively satisfying, it has its limitations. As we unpack her life situation, the adolescent feels little excitement at the prospect of continuing to live in her hometown. It turns out that she would really love to move to London, find a job as a hotel receptionist there and immerse herself in city life.

This is, however, out of the question for the adolescent as she could never leave her mother. The adolescent feels that her presence at home has enabled each of her siblings to leave home and create a life for themselves, as they knew that Shirley would have company and be looked after by the remaining siblings. Now though, there is nobody else at home but her and she would feel too guilty abandoning her mother. Juliette feels a burden of care for Shirley, despite the fact that her mum is in excellent health, is a strong and independent woman and has a great circle of friends. Juliette even jokes that her mother's social life is better than her own. I facilitate a conversation between them both in which Shirley expresses clearly and unequivocally her wish for her daughter to go and live her life to the full. She reassures Juliette that she does not need looking after. Shirley tells her daughter that it upsets her to think she is putting her life on hold unnecessarily. Mum positively rejects any idea that her daughter ought to live her life out of some misguided loyalty. Her claims that she is well able to take care of herself are convincing. Shortly after this joint session, Shirley talks to the four older girls and each of them reaches out to Juliette with support and encouragement. The adolescent's relief is tangible, and it is as if a burden has been lifted from her shoulders. Being the youngest, she felt stuck and had figured out that she would have to be the one to remain at home to mind her mother. Juliette needed to be liberated from this self-enforced family role in order for her to flourish once more. She started making plans for the move almost immediately. Unsurprisingly, the depressive edge evaporated.

Working with Parents

Where there is a specific issue in the adolescent's life, it is important to support parents to develop understanding and sensitivity in relation to their adolescent's experience. The primary enterprise with parents is creating the ground conditions for them to become more receptive. Deep, intensive strategy work is not typically necessary given that developmental process is not figural.

Fourteen-year-old John is the eldest of Derek and Helen's two children. His younger brother, Chris, has severe autism and requires constant care and supervision. Helen has reduced her working hours as a nurse to be available to attend to Chris's complex needs, whilst Derek is struggling to keep his business afloat in challenging economic times. Both parents are understandably and necessarily preoccupied. John is a resourceful and helpful adolescent and very easy to parent. However, recently he seems a bit flat. His grades have slipped, and he is not himself. During our first one-to-one meeting, John tells me that a number of months ago he came across a hospital letter addressed to his father with an appointment scheduled for a colonoscopy. Since that day, he has convinced himself that his dad is dying of cancer. This is checked out with parents and Derek reassures his son that this is not a sinister medical issue at all, but part of the process of a recent diagnosis of coeliac disease. Apart from needing to carefully attend to his diet, he is otherwise in great health. John starts to sob with relief and dad reaches out and hugs him. I encourage dad to sit right next to John on the large beanbag. He does so and puts his arm around his son who leans into him. John's yearnings have surfaced, and he is in a different space than he was during the initial assessment meeting where he assured everyone he was fine and did not need anything from his parents. With this tenderness between them, the focus of our conversation now shifts to their relationship.

John doesn't get to see his dad half as much as he would like and misses his contact. Derek is moved to learn of the depth of impact family dynamics have on John and has underestimated how important he is in his son's life. He realises that he needs to create more space for John and commits to them hanging out more together. Derek unwinds by playing golf and watching rugby and he involves John in these activities now. He starts teaching John to play golf and rather than going to the pub to watch the rugby with his mates, father and son watch together at home. In addition, Derek makes a point of popping into John's room every evening to have a chat with him and texting him more regularly when he is at work, just to say hello or send a funny meme. These small gestures make all the difference in the world.

Next time I see Helen, who has also managed to find some pockets of space for John, she reports that her son is *'the happiest boy'* and that he is *'in brilliant form'*. By our third session, John and I really have very little to talk about and the therapy is done. For so many parents in today's world, life transpires in ways which create dislocation from their directional teenage children who appear to be doing just fine. Creating deeper receptivity is the therapist's task in these instances and is generally not difficult to accomplish, unless the parent demonstrates an entrenched character style.

The Impulsive Parent

Nineteen-year-old Mari grew up in a violent, alcoholic household. Her parents, who both have alcohol issues, separated a decade ago though have a pattern of intermittently getting back together until the violence and drinking get out of hand again and the separation is reinstated once more. Other siblings try to intervene and have become enmeshed, though Mari remains singularly focused on her own life. She has learned to be hyper-independent and has difficulty trusting others and taking support. The adolescent has always been a largely directional person, focusing on her studies and sporting interests as a way of distracting herself from the chaos of home life. She is determined to create a bright and meaningful future for herself. However, Mari recently failed a module in her undergraduate study programme and broke down in tears when speaking with a lecturer who recognised that she was overwhelmed and recommended she speak to someone. When I inform Mari that I prefer to meet with parents and the young person together at the outset, she lets me know that this will not happen under any circumstances.

During our initial meeting the adolescent declares that she has no idea what she is doing here and doesn't feel the need to be in therapy, however she has promised the lecturer that she would attend at least once. We speak about her family dynamics and I sense that Mari is trusting me more than she thought she might. I name and appreciate her hyper-independent posture, offering my hunch that whilst she has endured much adversity in her young life, perhaps the real challenge for her, if she were to stay, would be allowing me to support her. She smiles and softens.

The adolescent decides to come back again and over the course of the next couple of years, we unpack her experience of being reared by traumatising parents and the ongoing imprint of this in her life. Mari views her father as still a teenager in many ways and eventually decides to stop seeing him. She has grown tired of his moods, drinking and rudeness. There is an initial backlash from siblings, though the adolescent holds her ground. Whilst remaining in relationship with and living in her mother's home, she lets go of her hope that mum will come to her senses, maintain sobriety and leave Mari's father for good. It is painful for the adolescent to grieve the loss that comes with this release of yearning in relation to her parents, and for a while she feels flooded. Taking the decision to cut ties with one's father and stepping back from trying to help one's struggling mother, whilst liberating, creates an enormous ache and is terribly lonely for any adolescent to choose to do.

Mari and I continue to work together, and I have not ever met with her parents. I agree with the adolescent that their participation would be both unhelpful and unnecessary, considering the adolescent's developmental stage and her level of resilience as well as the parents' active addictions and unhealthy relational dynamics. As is often the case with adolescents who configure directionally in the face of a traumatising family field, Mari is more evolved than her parents. Adolescents need a safe hand at their back to gently nurture, encourage and guide them. Preferably that is a parent's hand, though when this is not possible for whatever reason, other safe adults can make a transformative difference. The therapeutic relationship, and contact with benevolent others, continues to support the adolescent to feel safe, learn to trust and take support. Mari's hyper-independence started off as a fearful reaction to her parents: *I don't ever want to end up like them*. Now she is developing greater personal integrity so that her directionality is a statement about who she is and not merely a creative adjustment to traumatic parenting.

The Inhibitive Parent

Andrew and Stephanie had been unhappily married for years, made worse by the discovery of Andrew's affair a decade ago. The pair resolved to weather the storm and remain for the sake of their four children. They eventually separated during Freya's final year of secondary school. Freya, now attending university, is a directional adolescent and enjoys the freedom and independence of college life. She engages well in her study programme and loves her expanded social world. However, on discovering that her boyfriend has repeatedly cheated on her, she goes out to a club, gets very drunk, tells a friend she is going to kill herself and takes some pills. When her mother learns of the uncharacteristic incident, a referral is made for therapy.

Due to parental animosity, I meet separately with each parent and the young person as part of the contact assessment. During the meeting with Freya and her mother, I learn that the adolescent returns home every fortnight and spends most of the weekend in her mum's house. She considers this her home. Since the separation, the relationship between mother and daughter has taken a negative turn due to the fact that Stephanie talks a lot about her ex-husband and has recruited Freya as an emotional support. Mum is typically an attuned, if hyper-stressed, parent and this unhelpful boundary development is adjusted through some joint parent-adolescent psychotherapy sessions. I also encourage Stephanie to seek support elsewhere than from her children as she adjusts to the emotional, psychological, financial, legal, social and parental dynamics of marital separation. Recognising how their relationship has evolved in an unproductive manner, mum is willing to engage in a personal therapy process herself and this makes a considerable difference to her relationship with Freya.

When I meet Andrew, I am struck by how unconcerned he appears with regards to Freya's recent distress. Dad seems narcissistic and oblivious to his daughter's emotional world, downplaying her suffering and devaluing therapy as an unnecessary indulgence. Andrew offers his idea of what is likely to be the matter with Freya – she is very smart and could have done anything she wanted...but is wasting her life studying drama at college. Drama, for God's sake? If she had chosen law or medicine, like he advised, she would have a real career and excellent prospects ahead of her. Acting will give her no financial stability and more importantly, it will reflect badly on the family. Andrew compares the adolescent unfavourably to her siblings and his disapproval is unequivocal and hard-hitting. It is clear that Freya is treated like a narcissistic extension of her father and he is disappointed that she is not meeting the brief. I do not meet Andrew again during the psychotherapeutic process as to support parental attunement would require addressing his character structure. This would doubtless be a long-term undertaking, and Freya, not dad, is my client.

During individual work with Freya, it emerges that her boyfriend's infidelity triggered feelings of worthlessness, setting her on a rapid downward spiral which might have ended in catastrophe. As we explore the relationship with her father, the adolescent begins to connect the dots and now understands why she can be excessively self-critical. Freya recognises how her dad attempts to make her feel guilty for not caring since she doesn't spend much time with him. When she does see him, he talks mostly about himself. He never asks the adolescent how she is and doesn't talk to her about her life, unless to criticise her choices. Whilst she has demonstrated great courage in pursuing her artistic sensibilities and passion for drama, it has come at a cost – her father's disapproval. The adolescent comes to the awareness that her father is not interested in her as a unique person and realises that toeing the family line is the only way to make him proud. Freya's intuitive wisdom indicates that she will be miserable pursuing her father's agenda for her life and we experiment with how she can begin to tolerate his disapproval without absorbing shame. This supports her to adopt greater ownership of the life path she has chosen as Freya begins to appreciate her spiritedness and depth of integrity in refusing to live her life on another's terms. This process is liberating for Freya who continues to heal from growing up in a family atmosphere of constant evaluation and an expectation to be accommodating. The adolescent is finding her way.

Implications for Adulthood

Impulsive, inhibitive and directional configuration styles are modes of lifespace organisation during adolescence. These are influenced by brain functioning and the young person's emerging capacity to emotionally regulate, their propensity for insecure and self-derisory ruminating, and their capacity to find balance and apply bigger-picture thinking to their experience. Factors such as the level of parental attunement and depth of belonging within the peer world also make a qualitative difference to the adolescent's developmental journey.

For some young people, these configuration styles are distinct and recognisable stages through which they progress, as they demonstrate varying levels of intensity within each stage. Whilst the teenager continues to weave in and out of all three styles, one is more figural for a particular time during the adolescent years. Whilst parents and teachers may become concerned and frustrated, these are not fixed character and behaviour patterns. The young person will continue to advance developmentally, evolving into an increasingly mature and choiceful individual.

Many adolescents are more or less directional and cycle through the impulsive and inhibitive configuration styles episodically. Some adjust from one configuration style to another depending on the situation they find themselves in, for example, Cecilia demonstrates a directional approach to her part-time job. She is industrious, reliable and shows great initiative. However, the adolescent is inhibitive when it comes to her study, filled with anxiety about her upcoming exams and very uncertain about her third-level education choices. Meanwhile, at home she does nothing around the house and is prone to emotional outbursts. With her friends, she is the funny one who tends to overindulge on nights out. The degree of fluidity and lack of intensity with which she shifts between styles does not create too much concern for the adult world. And we will expect to see a gradual increase in directionality in Cecilia's presentation over time. She will come to resemble an adult more and more. Her development is on point.

Still others evidence a directional style of being which is a creative adjustment to a lifespace situation in which their needs are not being met, or where they feel compelled to adopt an adult role prematurely in their lives. Their directional configuration emerges from an experience of being overlooked. This often comes with a loss of personal integrity, as the young person remains attuned to the needs of others and disavows their own.

A number of adolescents become entrenched in one configuration style or other and develop a fixed way of relating within their lifespace. From the adolescent demographic, these extremely impulsive and inhibitive adolescents cause the greatest concern for adults and are the most likely candidates for therapy. The experience of parenting an adolescent who has become entrenched in an impulsive or inhibitive mode of being can be highly stressful and even traumatic for parents. Many of these young people remain entrenched as they leave adolescence behind and journey towards adulthood. Their development remains incomplete and unresolved, which in turn creates a host of issues when they become parents themselves. Attuned parenting requires a considerable degree of directional functioning.

Hopefully, by the time most individuals reach adulthood, they have attained a relatively directional status. However, no one remains directional at all times. We each have a wing of impulsivity or inhibition, some to a greater extent than others. As we grow and evolve, the influence of the adolescent years continues to reverberate throughout our lives, such is the significance of this critical developmental episode in the experience of being human.

Bibliography

American Psychiatric Association. (2013). *Diagnostic and statistical manual of mental disorders: Dsm-5*. American Psychiatric Association.

Barrett, L. F. (2017). *How emotions are made: The secret life of the brain*. New York: Mariner Books.

Beisser, A. R. (1970). *The Paradoxical Theory of Change*. Science and Behaviour Books.

Blakemore, S.-J. (2020). *Inventing ourselves: The secret life of the teenage brain*. PublicAffairs.

Bowlby, J. (1969). *Attachment and loss* (1st ed.). Basic Books.

boyd, d. (2015). *It's complicated: The social lives of networked teens*. Yale University Press.

Brackett, M. A. (2019). *Permission to feel: The power of emotional intelligence to achieve well-being and success*. New York: Celadon Books.

Chapman, L. (2014). *Neurobiologically informed trauma therapy with children and adolescents: Understanding mechanisms of change*. W.W. Norton & Company.

Cozolino, L. J. (2014). *The Neuroscience of Human Relationships: Attachment and the developing Social Brain*. New York: W.W. Norton & Company.

Crone, E. (2017). *The adolescent brain: Changes in learning, decision-making and social relations in the unique developmental period of adolescence*. Routledge.

Damasio, A. R. (1999). *The feeling of what happens: Body, emotion and the making of Consciousness*. New York: Harcourt.

Damour, L. (2017). *Untangled*. Atlantic Books.

Damour, L. (2020). *Under pressure: Confronting the epidemic of stress and anxiety in girls*. Atlantic Books.

Damour, L. (2023). *The emotional lives of teenagers: Raising connected, capable, and compassionate adolescents*. Ballantine Group.

Dines, G. (2012). *Pornland: How porn hijacked our sexuality*. Spinifex Press.

Eliot, L. (2010). *Pink brain, blue brain: How small differences grow into troublesome gaps – and what we can do about it*. New York: Mariner Books.

Feder, A., Cohen, H., Kim, J. J., Calderon, S., Charney, D. S., & Mathé, A. A. (2013). Understanding resilience. *Frontiers in Behavioral Neuroscience*, 7(10), 1–15. https://doi.org/10.3389/fnbeh.2013.00010

Francesetti, G., Gecele, M., & Roubal, J. (2013). *Gestalt therapy in clinical practice: From psychopathology to the aesthetics of contact*. Istituto di Gestalt.

Gopnik, A. (2016). *The gardener and the Carpenter: What the New Science of Child Development tells us about the relationship between parents and children*. Farrar, Straus and Giroux.

Greene, R. W. (2021). *The explosive child: A new approach for understanding and parenting easily frustrated, chronically inflexible children.* Harper.

Herman, J. L. (1992). *Trauma and recovery.* Basic Books.

Howe, D. (2000). *Attachment theory, child maltreatment and family support.* Palgrave.

Jackson Nakazawa, D. (2015). *Childhood disrupted: How your biography becomes your biology and how you can heal.* New York: Atria.

Jackson Nakazawa, D. (2022). *Girls on the Brink: Helping our daughters thrive in an era of increased anxiety, depression, and social media.* Harmony Books.

Jensen, F. (2016). *Teenage brain.* Harpercollins Canada.

Kegan, R. (2003). *In over our heads.* Harvard University Press.

Kerig, P., Ludlow, A., & Wenar, C. (2014). *Developmental psychopathology: From infancy through adolescence.* McGraw-Hill.

Kindlon, D., & Thompson, M. (1999). *Raising cain: Protecting the emotional lives of boys.* New York: Ballantine Books.

Kwee, J. L., & McBride, H. L. (2019). *Embodiment and eating disorders: Theory, research, prevention, and treatment.* Routledge.

Lee, R. G., & Wheeler, G. (2003). *The voice of shame.* Gestalt Press.

Lee, R., & Harris, N. (2011). *Relational Child, Relational Brain: Development and Therapy in Childhood and Adolescence (Evolution of Gestalt)* (1st ed.). Routledge, Taylor & Francis Group.

Maté, G. (2010). *In the Realm of Hungry Ghosts: Close Encounters with Addiction.* New York: North Atlantic Books.

McConville, M. (1995). *Adolescence: psychotherapy and the emergent self.* Josey-Bass.

McConville, M. (2021). *Failure to launch: Why your Twentysomething hasn't grown up... and what to do about it.* Putnam.

McKinnon, D. M. (1995). *The evolving self.* University Microfilms International.

McWilliams, N. (2011). *Psychoanalytic diagnosis.* Guilford Press.

Midgley, N., & Kennedy, E. (2011). Psychodynamic psychotherapy for children and adolescents: a critical review of the evidence base. *Journal of Child Psychotherapy, 37*(3), 232–260. https://doi.org/10.1080/0075417x.2011.614738

Midgley, N., Hayes, J., & Cooper, M. (2017). *Essential research findings in child and adolescent counselling and psychotherapy.* SAGE.

Miller, A., & Miller, A. (2008). *The drama of being a child: The search for the true self.* Virago.

Miller, L., & Barker, T. (2016). *The spiritual child: The new science on parenting for health and lifelong thriving.* Picador/St. Martin's Press.

Moorman, C. (1998). *Parent talk: Words that empower, words that wound: How to talk to your children in language that builds self-esteem and encourages responsibility.* Personal Power Press.

Natterson, C. (2020). *Decoding boys: New science behind the subtle art of Raising Sons.* New York: Balantine Books.

Orange, D. M. (2011). *The suffering stranger.* Routledge/Taylor & Francis Group.

Orenstein, P. (2016). *Girls & sex: Navigating the complicated new landscape.* Harper.

Papolos, D. F., & Papolos, J. (2010). *The bipolar child: The definitive and reassuring guide to Childhood's most misunderstood disorder.* Distributed by Paw Prints/Baker & Taylor.

Pattison, S., & Robson, M. (2018). *The handbook of counselling children and young people* (2nd ed.). Sage Publications.

Perry, B. D., & Winfrey, O. (2022). *What happened to you?: Conversations on trauma, resilience, and healing*. Bluebird.

Perry, P. (2020). *The book you wish your parents had read (and your children will be glad that you did)*. Penguin Life.

Pipher, M. B., & Gilliam, S. P. (2019). *Reviving Ophelia: Saving the selves of adolescent girls*. Riverhead Books.

Reyna, V. F. (2012). *The adolescent brain: Learning, reasoning, and decision making*. American Psychological Association.

Sadlier, R. (2022). *Let's talk; about relationships, sex and intimacy*. Gill Books.

Siegel, D. J. (2013). *Brainstorm*. Jeremy P. Tarcher/Penguin.

Siegel, D. J. (2020). *The developing mind: How relationships and the brain interact to shape who we are*. The Guilford Press.

Siegel, D. J., & Bryson, T. P. (2020). *The power of showing up: How parental presence shapes who our kids become and how their brains get wired*. Ballantine Books.

Simmons, R. (2019). *Enough as she is: How to help girls move beyond impossible standards of success to live healthy, happy, and fulfilling lives*. Harper.

Spear, L. P. (2010). *The behavioral neuroscience of adolescence*. W.W. Norton.

Starrs, B. (2014). Contact and despair: A Gestalt approach to adolescent trauma. *British Gestalt Journal, 23*(2), 28–37.

Starrs, B. (2019). *Adolescent psychotherapy: A radical relational approach*. Routledge.

Steinberg, L. (2015). *Age of opportunity: Lessons from the new science of adolescence*. New York: Harper.

Stern, D. N. (2006). *The interpersonal world of the infant: A view from psychoanalysis and development psychology*. Karnac.

Stixrud, W., & Johnson, N. (2018). *The Self-Driven Child*. New York: Viking.

Streeter, C. C., Gerbarg, P. L., Saper, R. B., Ciraulo, D. A., & Brown, R. P. (2012). Effects of yoga on the autonomic nervous system, gamma-aminobutyric-acid, and allostasis in epilepsy, depression, and post-traumatic stress disorder. *Medical Hypotheses, 78*(5), 571–579. https://doi.org/10.1016/j.mehy.2012.01.021

Tronick, E., & Gold, C. M. (2020). *The Power of discord: Why the ups and downs of relationships are the secret to building intimacy, resilience, and trust*. New York: Little, Brown/Spark.

Twenge, J. M. (2018). *Igen: Why today's super-connected kids are growing up less rebellious, more tolerant, less happy – and completely unprepared for adulthood (and what that means for the rest of us)*. Atria Books.

van der Kolk, B. A. (2005). Developmental Trauma Disorder: Toward a rational diagnosis for children with complex trauma histories. *Psychiatric Annals, 35*(5), 401–408. https://doi.org/10.3928/00485713-20050501-06

Van der Kolk, B. A. (2015). *The body keeps the score*. Penguin Books.

Waddell, M. (2019). *Inside lives: Psychoanalysis and the growth of the personality*. Routledge.

Walsh, J. (2018). *Adolescents and their social media narratives: A digital coming of age*. Routledge.

Wheeler, G. (2000). *Beyond individualism: Toward a new understanding of self, relationship, and experience*. Cambridge, MA: GIC Press.

Wheeler, G., & Axelsson, L. (2015). *Gestalt therapy*. American Psychological Association.

Index